SHARED FOUNDATIONS

Collaborate

SHARED FOUNDATIONS SERIES

SHARED FOUNDATIONS

Collaborate

MARY CATHERINE COLEMAN

CHICAGO | 2020

American Association
of School Librarians
TRANSFORMING LEARNING

ISBNs
978-0-8389-1915-6 (paper)
978-0-8389-1929-3 (PDF)
978-0-8389-1927-9 (ePub)
978-0-8389-1928-6 (Kindle)

Library of Congress Cataloging-in-Publication Data

Names: Coleman, Mary Catherine, 1976- author.
Title: Collaborate / Mary Catherine Coleman.
Description: Chicago : ALA Editions, 2020. | Series: Shared foundations | Includes bibliographical references and index. | Summary: "This book will make connections with the AASL Standards and approach the idea of collaboration from three areas: 1) Collaboration between school librarians and classroom educators to create library lessons and projects that meet library skills goals as well as classroom learning goals to create a collaborative experience for learners that flows through multiple spaces and creates a learning foundation for skills and ideas. 2) Collaboration skills for Learners. It is essential that learners learn to be collaborative and know how to work with others, share ideas and receive feedback. This book will share practical ideas and plans on how school librarians can weave the development of this essential skill into projects and lessons. 3) Space. The school library is the heart of the school and it is imperative that the space fosters a culture of collaboration in the physical space but also allows for the time, space, and freedom for learners to collaborate. This book will look at how the physical library space and the culture and philosophy of the library can help to cultivate collaboration in learners and educators"— Provided by publisher.
Identifiers: LCCN 2019026652 (print) | LCCN 2019026653 (ebook) | ISBN 9780838919156 (paperback) | ISBN 9780838919279 (epub) | ISBN 9780838919286 (kindle edition) | ISBN 9780838919293 (pdf)
Subjects: LCSH: School libraries—United States. | School librarian participation in curriculum planning—United States. | Student participation in curriculum planning United States. | Libraries and schools—United States.
Classification: LCC Z675.S3 C64 2019 (print) | LCC Z675.S3 (ebook) | DDC 027.80973—dc23
LC record available at https://lccn.loc.gov/2019026652
LC ebook record available at https://lccn.loc.gov/2019026653

⊗ This paper meets the requirements of ANSI/NISO Z39.48-1992 (Permanence of Paper).

Printed in the United States of America
24 23 22 21 20   5 4 3 2 1

Purchases of AASL Publications fund advocacy, leadership, professional development, and standards initiatives for school librarians nationally.

ALA Editions purchases fund advocacy, awareness, and accreditation programs for library professionals worldwide.

SHARED FOUNDATION III
Collaborate

Work effectively with others
to broaden perspectives
and work toward common goals.

Contents

Acknowledgments

What I know about collaboration and development of the mindset of collaboration in learners in a school library and education community is all due to an amazing group of colleagues and my team.

Thank you to Sarah Beebe, Annette Lesak, Eric Rampson, and Seth Bacon—all my squad and team at the Francis W. Parker School library. They are creative, thoughtful partners in developing an innovative and forward-thinking school library. Thank you to my fellow teachers and educators, including Mike McPharlin, Bev Greenberg, Maureen Cuesta, Amy Przygoda, Kate Tabor, Alex Bearman, and Elizabeth Joebgen. Collaboration in a school library is not possible without fellow educators who are willing to sit down and talk and be open to new ideas.

Series Introduction

The Shared Foundations series from the American Association of School Librarians (AASL) examines the six Shared Foundations that anchor the comprehensive approach to teaching and learning in the *National School Library Standards for Learners, School Librarians, and School Libraries.* The Shared Foundations—Inquire, Include, Collaborate, Curate, Explore, and Engage—represent the core concepts that all learners, school librarians, and school libraries develop and promote in their K–12 learning environment.

Each of the six books in this series is dedicated to the deep exploration of a single Shared Foundation. Although each of the Shared Foundations supports its own inherent priorities, it cannot be implemented in isolation. The writing process used by the authors created a series of books that, like the AASL Standards Frameworks, are unique and yet parallel each other. Common elements are found throughout the series:

- A balance between theoretical discussion, practical strategies, and implementation examples, promoting reflection and creativity
- Development of the Competencies and Alignments for the Learner, School Librarian, and School Library in all four Domains—Think, Create, Share, and Grow
- Differences in application and assessment across grades K–12, promoting a growth mindset and envisioning outcomes for all learners, whether student learners, school librarians, or other educators
- An emphasis on personalized learning experiences, project-based learning, and authenticity of learning and projects
- Challenges addressed, illustrating ways to implement the Shared Foundations in various environments and levels of support

Questions for the Reflective Practitioner conclude each chapter, allowing readers to consider the application of concepts specific to their own learning communities and stimulate nuanced professional conversations. For ease of reference, readers also will find the AASL Standards Integrated Framework for the relevant Shared Foundation included in this work.

AASL and its series authors hope that this immersive and dedicated examination of the Shared Foundations will help school library professionals deepen their understandings, broaden their perspectives, make connections for personal relevance, and innovate and reflect on their practice with a professional community.

For more information about the *National School Library Standards*, and to access the latest implementation assistance resources, visit standards.aasl.org.

Domain	LEARNER DOMAINS AND COMPETENCIES	SCHOOL LIBRARIAN DOMAINS AND COMPETENCIES
A. Think	**Learners identify collaborative opportunities by:** 1. Demonstrating their desire to broaden and deepen understandings. 2. Developing new understandings through engagement in a learning group. 3. Deciding to solve problems informed by group interaction.	**School librarians facilitate collaborative opportunities by:** 1. Challenging learners to work with others to broaden and deepen understandings. 2. Scaffolding enactment of learning-group roles to enable the development of new understandings within a group. 3. Organizing learner groups for decision making and problem solving.
B. Create	**Learners participate in personal, social, and intellectual networks by:** 1. Using a variety of communication tools and resources. 2. Establishing connections with other learners to build on their own prior knowledge and create new knowledge.	**School librarians demonstrate the importance of personal, social, and intellectual networks by:** 1. Modeling the use of a variety of communication tools and resources. 2. Cultivating networks that allow learners to build on their own prior knowledge and create new knowledge.
C. Share	**Learners work productively with others to solve problems by:** 1. Soliciting and responding to feedback from others. 2. Involving diverse perspectives in their own inquiry processes.	**School librarians promote working productively with others to solve problems by:** 1. Demonstrating how to solicit and respond to feedback from others. 2. Advocating and modeling respect for diverse perspectives to guide the inquiry process.
D. Grow	**Learners actively participate with others in learning situations by:** 1. Actively contributing to group discussions. 2. Recognizing learning as a social responsibility.	**School librarians foster active participation in learning situations by:** 1. Stimulating learners to actively contribute to group discussions. 2. Creating a learning environment in which learners understand that learning is a social responsibility.

SCHOOL LIBRARY DOMAINS AND ALIGNMENTS	The school library facilitates the Key Commitment to and Competencies of COLLABORATE	Domain
The school library facilitates opportunities to integrate collaborative and shared learning by: 1. Partnering with other educators to scaffold learning and organize learner groups to broaden and deepen understanding. 2. Leading inquiry-based learning opportunities that enhance the information, media, visual, and technical literacies of all members of the school community.		**A. Think**
The school library's policies ensure that school librarians are active participants in development, evaluation, and improvement of instructional and program resources with the school librarian by: 1. Consistently engaging with the school community to ensure that the school library resources, services, and standards align with the school's mission. 2. Participating in district, building, and department or grade-level curriculum development and assessment on a regular basis. 3. Including the school community in the development of school library policies and procedures.		**B. Create**
The school library provides opportunities for school librarians to connect and work with the learning community by: 1. Facilitating diverse social and intellectual learner networks. 2. Designing and leading professional-development opportunities that reinforce the impact of the school library's resources, services, and programming on learners' academic learning and educators' effectiveness. 3. Promoting and modeling the importance of information-use skills by publicizing to learners, staff, and the community available services and resources; serving on school and district-wide committees; and engaging in community and professional activities.		**C. Share**
The school library supports active learner participation by: 1. Creating and maintaining a learning environment that supports and stimulates discussion from all members of the school community. 2. Demonstrating and reinforcing the idea that information is a shared resource.		**D. Grow**

Introduction:
The Complexity of Collaborate

In the school library, a learner shares an idea during a class discussion on the topic of water conservation. Another learner raises a hand and says, "Building on what Sloane said about clean water, I think . . ." and shares ideas and connections to the topic related to the classmate's ideas. In another space in the school library, learners are gathered in a small group, planning and designing a project, collecting resources, and sharing ideas to define the problem and present solutions. Learners are listening and sharing with each other. In a study room, a learner who made a presentation is reading feedback received from the educator, peers, and a local expert who visited the class. At tables across the library, educators are gathered to learn about a new piece of technology they are interested in incorporating into their curriculum. All these learners are engaging in collaborative work.

Collaboration is complex and layered. Collaboration includes whole-group discussions, small-group work, and even individual work. It takes time and space to develop the skills of a collaborator to "work effectively with others to broaden perspectives and work toward common goals" (AASL 2018, 85). Collaboration is about listening and learning from others. It includes communicating and sharing knowledge and ideas, as well as defining and solving problems. Collaboration includes negotiating and compromising as part of accomplishing shared goals. Collaboration is about empathy for others and welcoming diverse perspectives to understand a challenge and reach a solution. Developing the mindset of collaboration takes time and space. Learners need the opportunity to collaborate, fail at the process, learn from it, and try again.

National School Library Standards: A Call for Collaboration

The *National School Library Standards for Learners, School Librarians, and School Libraries* call for school librarians to create a culture of collaboration that includes not just learners but fellow educators, administrators, and the larger school community. The school librarian is in the position to be a powerful force behind that culture of collaboration. The role of the school librarian enables working with other educators in the building, across grade levels and disciplines. School librarians usually see multiple, if not all, grade levels, and in many cases the school librarian has connections across schools and districts in a way that other educators do not. The diverse roles that school librarians enact present opportunities to delve deeply into the Shared Foundation of Collaborate—one of six Shared Foundations (Inquire, Include, Collaborate, Curate, Explore, and Engage) anchoring AASL's *National School Library Standards*—and to identify opportunities for school librarians to establish and shape a culture of collaboration in the school community that benefits learners, fellow educators, and other stakeholders.

The AASL Standards state that "an effective school library results in learners' increased academic achievement and improved educator effectiveness" (AASL 2018, 90). A cornerstone of that improved educator effectiveness is the school librarian's driving of the sharing of resources, including technology, research, and information-literacy skills to benefit learners. It also includes leading professional development at the school. Professional development led by the school librarian is an effective way to ensure that the school library remains front and center within the school culture and that the school librarian is a leader in the advancement and innovation that are happening at the school. The role of the school librarian is still rooted in the foundations of literacy, research, and information-seeking skills, but because we are well into the second decade of the twenty-first century, the role of the school librarian has expanded to include modeling and teaching Internet research skills, safe use of social media, characteristics of good digital citizenship, and knowledge about emerging technologies and devices. School librarians and school libraries are also playing a key role in the maker movement. Followers of this movement provide a space for designing, innovating, and tinkering with hard materials, such as 3-D printers and laser cutters, as well as soft materials, like cardboard and yarn. This movement is changing the physical space of the school library. Being at the center of an evolving educational landscape puts school librarians in a unique position to influence and advance the changing culture and offers the amazing opportunity to incorporate the Shared Foundation of Collaborate in meaningful, far-reaching ways.

A Winding Path to Successful Collaboration

The AASL *National School Library Standards* provide an integrated framework for the implementation of their Shared Foundations in three areas: learners, school librarians, and school libraries. The Domains of Think, Create, Share, and Grow further define specific Competencies for learners and school librarians and Alignments for school libraries. The AASL Standards Integrated Framework for the Shared Foundation Collaborate can be found immediately following the Series Introduction to this book. The challenge for school librarians in implementing the Shared Foundation Collaborate within their communities is that the path to developing a culture of collaboration is not linear. The school librarian's collaborative work with fellow educators in designing lessons flows into the learners' engagement in collaborative opportunities, which are connected to the space and time available in the school library for collaboration. Also, as learners and fellow educators develop the skills of collaborators, the collaboration in which they engage becomes more complex. Collaboration looks different at different stages, with different age groups, and in different school communities. All these aspects of collaboration play a role in the school librarian's design and plan to implement the *National School Library Standards* and develop collaboration skills in the school community.

The Intersection of Learner, School Librarian, and School Library

The organization of this book approaches the Shared Foundation of Collaborate, the Domains, Competencies, and Alignments not as a checklist to follow but as a Venn Diagram. This approach illustrates the intersections within the AASL Standards Integrated Framework (figure I.1) and will demonstrate how to recognize the shared responsibilities of the learner, school librarian, and school library in developing a culture of collaboration.

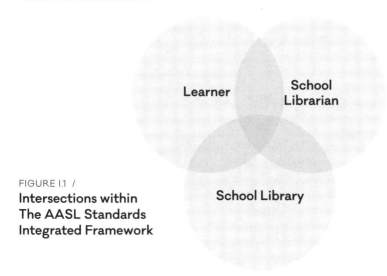

FIGURE I.1 /
Intersections within The AASL Standards Integrated Framework

Each section of this book covers an aspect of the Shared Foundation Collaborate. The first part looks at the role of collaboration in school librarian-led professional development, connections to the mission of the school, and the work of the school librarian as a co-designer of projects and lessons with fellow educators to connect the curriculum of the school library with the curricular work of the school. The second part of the book dives more deeply into developing the skills of a collaborator in learners and the development of those skills within different age groups. The chapters in the final part explore the role that school library spaces, both physical and metaphorical, play in the development of a collaborative culture. Even though each section tackles an area of the *National School Library Standards* by focusing on the learner, school librarian, or school library, the intersections with the other areas are documented. Each chapter includes examples demonstrating the connected Competencies and Alignments in action to allow readers to see these intersections. The goal is for readers to recognize the interconnected nature of these three areas in creating a culture of collaboration within a school community as well as the complexities of collaboration when developing this mindset in learners and educator partners. The hope is that this book will help readers see their own paths to developing implementation plans based on their school communities and patrons and to developing the skills of collaboration in learners, fellow educators, administrators, and other members of the school community.

PART I

The School Librarian as the Architect of Collaboration

1

Designing Collaborative Educator Learning Environments

atie Martin, author of *Learner-Centered Innovation: Spark* *Curiosity, Ignite Passion and Unleash Genius,* asked the question, "If we don't prioritize authentic and relevant learning experiences for educators, how can we ensure our students have deeper learning experiences?" (Martin 2018, 9). If the goal is to have learners engage in authentic, collaborative work that is creative, is inquiry based, and allows for critical thinking, educators must engage in the same work. Martin went on to say, "If we want to change how students learn, we must change how teachers learn" (Martin 2018, 9). For school librarians and fellow educators to develop the mindset of collaboration in learners, the school librarian and classroom educators need to develop the skills of a collaborator as well. For that to happen, educators need to participate in collaborative work with fellow educators. Because their work crosses content areas and grade levels, school librarians are in a position to lead collaborative professional development for the whole school community. School librarians can be a driving force in rethinking what professional development looks like at the school and district levels and follow Martin's directive to change how educators learn. When educators exemplify collaborative learning through professional development, they learn to teach the Competencies of Collaborate. This modeling and understanding are key to changing how learners learn and are an important element in the AASL Standards, having a tangible impact on student learning and growth.

Modeling Collaboration through Professional Development

The AASL Standards call for "school librarians to connect and work with the learning community by designing and leading professional-development opportunities that reinforce the impact of the school library's resources, services, and programming on learners' academic learning and educators' effectiveness" (AASL 2018, School Library III.C.2.). For enduring results from professional development that promotes the school library, participants must engage with fellow educators in collaborative learning activities that require them to use the resources, services, and programs offered through the school library. If school librarians and other educators want learners to be collaborators, then all educators in the school must participate in similar collaborative learning experiences in their own professional learning. If school librarians and fellow educators want learners to be collaborative critical thinkers and risk takers, then all educators must also model these characteristics. Just as student learners require a safe space to experiment, fail, and grow, so do educators. Professional development is one of the learning environments of educators and offers a safe space for them to build collaborative competencies and explore. By designing and offering professional development that incorporates collaboration and new and inspired ways of engaging with other educators and members of the school community, school librarians position themselves to foster a culture of collaboration while leading educational innovation through the school library.

Educators must engage in new learning environments and activities so that they can model that learning for student learners. In addition, the constantly changing educational landscape requires that the school community innovate and change. School librarians can provide those opportunities. By being the architects of a "learning environment that supports and stimulates discussion from all members of the school community" (AASL 2018, School Library III.D.1.), school librarians can collaborate to bring different disciplines together, have an impact on the larger school curriculum, and implement the AASL Standards across the school learning environment. To accomplish these goals, school librarians need to be innovative, too, in their planning and sharing of professional development through the school library.

COLLABORATE IN ACTION: CONSTRUCTING COLLABORATIVE LEARNING COHORTS

When the library department at my school merged with the technology education program and we combined our curricula (see chapter 3 for details of how this change was made), we wanted to reach out and offer professional development to educators that would connect our new department with the school's mission of fostering and demonstrating a growth mindset, cultural competence, and intellectual curiosity. Our objective was to spread the development of these mindsets beyond the walls of the school library and the computer lab into the classroom and into the curriculum. We wanted to collaborate with other educators to align the school's mission with the goals of the school library department, including empowering makers, teaching and supporting digital literacy, guiding learners to use technology effectively, and innovating in support of teaching and learning. When we brainstormed about how to engender enthusiasm for these goals, professional development was at the top of the list. However, we wanted to expand professional development beyond the traditional systems of talking at a meeting or sending out an e-mail with resources. We had to rethink how to reach educators and imagine more-engaging ways to communicate so that change could be enacted through a process reflecting the way learners learn.

We wanted the professional development to be inquiry based and educator driven. We wanted to create opportunities for educators to have conversations about and examine aspects of their curriculum. We wanted groups of educators to share differing ideas and receive feedback from peers to help participants' work with learners evolve. The goal was to lead "inquiry-based learning opportunities that enhance the information, media, visual, and technical literacies of all members of the school community" (AASL 2018, School Library III.A.2.). When we started brainstorming about making significant changes to the way professional development was presented, we knew we would need administrative support to make this collaborative approach work within the educators' complicated schedules. We mapped out a plan. What if we offered learning cohorts for educators? In these cohorts, educators would be organized by their interests in making changes or adding to their curriculum. Participants would be asked to change or try at least one new thing in their curriculum during the school year and would meet several times that year to talk about their ideas and receive feedback from others as they experimented with their teaching practice. This format allowed us to bring together educators from all over the school, "facilitating diverse social and intellectual learner networks" (AASL 2018, School Librarian III.C.1.).

An important aspect of this professional development was that the school librarians and the technology education teachers would also be working on their own projects and ideas. Nobody was in a sit-and-listen professional development cohort. All educators—including members of our new department—would be learning and growing with peers. In this way, everyone was engaged in the process, everyone was trying something new, and everyone was receiving feedback. By including ourselves in the learning process, we were engaged in the professional development with all our co-educators. Our inclusion in the process helped to build a collaborative learning group in which we developed relationships and leaned on each other. School librarians are experts in many areas, but room always exists to grow and change and gain new perspectives about what we are doing. As much as we want to share innovative ways of teaching and learning, we need to step back and rethink our own curriculum as well. School librarians need to be lifelong learners along with other educators and our student learners. Modeling and engaging in collaboration ourselves are the best ways to cultivate a learner-centered and collaborative learning environment.

Think: Drafting Our Blueprint

The team spent days mapping out how the year would unfold, how many cohort meetings would be held, what they would look like, and what the work would entail for all participants to be successful in the process. The team used the idea of journey maps from the business and design world to help design the experience for participants over the course of the yearlong cohorts. In the business world, a customer journey map "is a visualization of the process that a person goes through to accomplish a goal. It's used for understanding and addressing customer needs and pain points" (Kaplan 2016). The goal of a journey map is to dive deeply into the customer experience by using elements of storytelling and visualization to anticipate customer needs, allowing designers to create a more worthwhile product or experience to better serve the customer. In the case of professional development planning, the journey map focused on the experience that an educator may have throughout the year of activities, and the designers of that experience wanted it to be as rewarding, enduring, and positive for the educator as possible. We wanted to visualize the story of what that experience would be to better plan for all types of educator participants. We wanted to lay the groundwork for a successful year of "challenging learners to work with others to broaden and deepen understandings" (AASL 2018, School Librarian III.A.1.). Anticipating challenges and planning ahead were key to collaborative learning experiences for cohort members. The journey map included four categories:

1. Actions: What would participants be working on? Where would they be in their curriculum design?
2. Emotions: What would participants be feeling? How would the different challenges of the school year schedule impact their process?
3. Questions: What questions or concerns would participants have at different points in the year?
4. Touchpoints: What would the members of the school library department be doing at different times to help the participants' process? How would the school library department members be engaging with the educators to help keep them on track and moving forward in the process? How could school library department members use e-mails, Google Drive Team folders, and the like to stay connected?

The team used a whiteboard to draw a table charting these four points on the journey map following the school calendar and thinking about what these categories would look like in each month of the school year (table 1.1). This map helped the team to better plan for the yearlong process, anticipate challenges so that the team could pivot and adjust as the work of each cohort evolved, and, during what we knew would be a critical next step, develop a strategy for presenting our cohort model to the administration to gain support.

Create: Getting Administration on Board

For this professional development to succeed, we needed school leaders to support the cohort model and grant educators time within their schedules to collaborate. The school had recently identified three learner qualities that the community determined were essential for educators to focus on developing in our learners: a growth mindset, cultural competency, and intellectual curiosity. Our team knew that aligning our plan with these qualities would increase our chances of securing leadership support. As part of our design plan for the professional development cohorts, educators who participated would document their activities and note connections between their work and one or more of these essential learner qualities. Educators would have documentation to demonstrate achievement of their professional learning goals, and administrators could clearly see how the learning cohorts connected to the mission and goals of the school.

This element was key to gaining administrative support. By showing that the learning cohorts connected in concrete ways to the goals of the school, we were "consistently engaging with the school community to ensure that the school library resources, services, and standards align with the school's mission" (AASL 2018, School Library III.B.1.). Our plan positioned the school library as an essential component in achieving the school's mission of cultivating the essential learner qualities in student learners. The administration agreed to excuse educators participating in the learning cohorts from attending faculty meetings throughout the school year. This arrangement was a great success for us because we were able to give our participants the time needed to collaborate and work in their learning cohorts. The use of faculty meeting time ensured that educators from different departments and divisions would be able to participate and that the school librarians would be "participating in district, building, and department or grade-level curriculum development and assessment" (AASL 2018, School Library III.B.2.). Participants would be using time that was already on educators' calendars; busy educators did not have to commit additional time to participate, a circumstance that increased their willingness to join a cohort. By providing the faculty the time to engage in this work, we were also providing opportunities for "cultivating networks that allow learners to build on their own prior knowledge and create new knowledge" (AASL 2018, School Librarian III.B.2.).

Share: Reaching Out to Faculty

The next step involved soliciting feedback from educators about the topics they were interested in exploring while focusing on the core mindsets for learners on which the school focused: growth mindset, cultural competency, and intellectual curiosity. The school library team hosted a meeting to present the idea of the cohorts to the faculty. In groups we discussed time and space to work on curriculum and prompted educators to think about something they have always wanted to explore

TABLE 1.1 / **Educator experience journey map**

Timeline	September	October
Actions What are participants doing?	• Introduce the plan for the year to the cohort • Getting to know other members of the cohort • Brainstorm different project ideas and share with each other in the cohort	• Brainstorming activity to work through project ideas • To-do list: Map out everyone's plans • I like/I wish/I wonder feedback routine for each member's project ideas • Listen to others and keep an open mind
Emotions What are participants feeling?	• Open to possibilities • Energized for the new school year • Ready to get going • Determined • Maybe a little nervous about this process	• Settled into the school year a bit • Comfortable with learners in their classes • Supported by facilitators in cohort • Still excited and ready to engage in this process • More comfortable with the process
Questions What are participants asking?	• What should I focus on? • Where do I fit in this cohort? • What do I need to get started? • What are the expectations for cohort members? • What kind of access do I have to the facilitators? • What is the meeting schedule? • Is there a budget for projects? • What happens if I have to miss a meeting?	• Will we have enough time in meetings to work on individual projects? • Will I be able to produce something, and what if I don't? • What are the expectations for documentation of my project and process?
Touchpoints What are *we* doing?	**Set up** Google Folder, share with group members (to document work, artifacts, etc.) **Have** a group norm conversation—perhaps we can pull from our norms and create something **Manage Expectations**: Set realistic goals; avoid and re-steer conversation about things that are unrealistic and funnel that energy into things that are realistic	**Track** project ideas with templates in the Google Folder **Set up** follow-up meetings/check-ins with individual cohort members between meetings **Create** shared calendar to help members stay on track and be aware of when other cohort members' projects are planned **Remind** cohort members that the process is more important than the final output and focus on that

November	December
Designing • Flushing out cohort members' ideas and plans • Focused on a project or lesson to work on • Time to work on plans and ideas • Sharing ideas and feedback with cohort members	**Designing** • Spending time working on project design • Implementation and reflection • Feedback from cohort if needed
• Gaining traction in curriculum and with learners; confident and moving forward • Starting to feel a little overwhelmed as the semester is coming to a close and upcoming breaks create stress	• Not much • Excited that this project actually might happen • Stressed with winter break and all the activity leading up to break • A little stressed that half the year is done
• Am I on the right track with my project? • Am I still in this process? • Are there roadblocks in my project work? What are ways to overcome these roadblocks?	• How can I improve my design? • Do I really need all this design time? • What resources do I need to make this project happen? • What are my next steps? • If I implemented my lesson, what are my next steps, a next iteration I can do to improve?
Give feedback to all cohort members to help them stay on track **Help** cohort members stay focused and make any adjustments **Offer** advice and suggestions to overcome roadblocks that cohort members are encountering	**Check in** with cohort members on progress **Offer** assistance with any resources or materials needed **Refresh and Refocus** cohort for January; help cohort members plan for next steps **Remind** cohort members about documentation for final share-out

(continued)

TABLE 1.1 / **Educator experience journey map** *(continued)*

Timeline	January	February
Actions What are participants doing?	**Designing** • Spending time working on project design • Implementation and reflection • Feedback from cohort if needed	**Designing** • Spending time working on project design • Implementation and reflection • Feedback from cohort if needed
Emotions What are participants feeling?	• Impatient and ready to get project going with learners • Stressed to finish	• Impatient and ready to get project going with learners • Stressed to finish • Fingers crossed
Questions What are participants asking?	• Am I heading in the right direction? • Do I have everything I need to implement and produce something? • What will happen when I test my project/lesson? • How do I collect feedback from my learners/ colleagues?	• What is the best audience to test my lesson/project on? • Do I have my plan set, and am I ready to move forward? • Do I have everything in place to document this process?
Touchpoints What are *we* doing?	**Feedback** for all cohort members on their projects and lessons **Time and Space** for cohort members to finalize projects and lesson materials, resources, and plans **Update** shared folders for documentation **Remind** cohort members about documentation for final share-out	**Test** lessons and project ideas **Feedback** for all cohort members on their projects and lessons **Time and Space** for cohort members to finalize projects and lesson materials, resources, and plans **Update** shared folders for documentation

March	April	May
Prototype • Fine-tuning and finishing the prototype for lesson or project • Beginning to work on share-out if ready to move to that	**Prototype** • Fine-tuning and finishing the prototype for lesson or project • Beginning to work on share-out if ready to move to that	Sharing
• Sweating out final prep • Fingers crossed • Feeling out of time	• Nervous • Anticipation	• Excited • Proud • Happy to be done
• Will I have time to revisit and rework or make changes? • How will I handle the results that my test provides? • How did I do? • How did my learners do?	• What worked? • Did I do this process right? • What would I change?	• Was this process worth it? • What would I change for next year? • Did my learners benefit from this process? • Did I benefit from this process?
Support cohort members and provide what is needed to feel successful **Check in** with all members individually to make sure they have completed work or have a timeline for completion that is reasonable **Focus** on the share-out and what cohort members will share with the faculty about the experience	**Share** plans and support to complete **Reflection** on the process **Success** comes in lots of formats, and design is an iterative process	**Reflection** on the process for the learners and the cohort members **Reflection** for the facilitators on the process, their process, and their support **Suggestions** for next year—what worked, and what might you change for next year

in their work, if only they were given time. By asking fellow educators to contribute to the topics for the learning cohorts, we were "advocating and modeling respect for diverse perspectives to guide the inquiry process" (AASL 2018, School Librarian III.C.2.). After the faculty had several days to think about options, they completed a Google form to identify a topic they would like to explore. The school library team then sorted and connected topics and ideas, creating four cohorts.

- **Group 1** focused on incorporating new technologies into their curriculum, with special attention on materials offered in the school library's new maker-space.
- **Group 2** looked at ways to better document learners' learning and emphasize the learning process over the end product to better reflect on the skills of collaboration, critical thinking, and learning from failure.
- **Group 3** looked at perspective and voice in their curriculum and ways to better incorporate the literature and history of traditionally marginalized or silenced voices. Participants' goal was to ensure that student learners heard all perspectives while recognizing that the voices of many have been silenced.
- **Group 4** looked at incorporating social-emotional learning practices into their curriculum to better help learners handle difficult situations by developing better listening, communication, and collaboration skills.

Discovering the interests and passions of our fellow educators aided our team in "facilitating diverse social and intellectual learner networks" (AASL 2018, School Library III.C.1.) that would advance educators' practice and make deeper connections with the work of the school library. Once we established the learning cohorts, we set out to develop routines and practices to ensure that the time the educators were given was used to its fullest and to foster a learning culture in which all participants could be successful.

Share and Grow: Cohort Meetings

The school library team established a tentative agenda for the yearlong cohort teams to follow. Facilitators from the school library team started the meetings with each cohort by establishing group norms so that everyone had a voice.

The norms focused on how and when participants would share their projects and on how much of the time would be spent in discussion versus individual work time. Each group also set the norm of using the I like/I wish/I wonder feedback routine. After a participant shared a unit or project idea, others in the group would respond with an aspect they liked (I like), an area in which they saw challenges (I wish), and an extension idea for the plan (I wonder). Setting group norms and gaining feedback from participants ensured that we were "creating and maintaining a learning environment that supports and stimulates discussion from all members of the school community" (AASL 2018, School Library III.D.1.) while "demonstrating

Getting Started: A Glance at the Year

The school library team established a brief agenda for the year. The agenda was tentative, giving room for the cohorts to determine some of the items and timeline depending on their work. The yearlong agenda focused on items the school library department determined were essential for every group to engage in regardless of the focus of the cohort.

1. **Collaborative Relationships**
   a. Establishing norms within the cohort
   b. Checking in throughout the year with each cohort member to gauge how individuals are feeling about the process and determine the best way to support them
   c. Observation by facilitators of conversations and products

2. **Design Curriculum**
   a. Producing a product
   b Documenting the process (helps with sharing)

3. **Needs Assessment**
   a. Creating a rubric or checklist to assess the needs of the learner—Educator's True North
   b. Connecting with the learner characteristics identified and supported by the Francis W. Parker School (growth mindset, cultural competency, or intellectual curiosity)

4. **Prototype and Test**
   a. Implementing in some form to test your idea
   b. Setting of reflection questions based on testing

5. **Reflect and Share Product and Process with Faculty**

how to solicit and respond to feedback from others" (AASL 2018, School Librarian III.C.1.). Group norms and the use of the feedback routine were also ways of "stimulating learners to actively contribute to group discussions" (AASL 2018, School Librarian III.D.1.). We set timelines for sharing and working together (table 1.2). Finally, we emphasized that a final share-out would occur at the end of the school year. The share-out was intended to show the administration that the process was a worthwhile use of faculty time by highlighting the process and the products, to share educator work with the larger community to spark interest and ideas, and, we hoped, to encourage participation of more faculty in the next iteration of the cohorts.

TABLE 1.2 / **Example timeline for learner documentation cohort**

This example timeline developed by the Learner Documentation cohort group demonstrates the overarching monthly stages followed by all cohort groups throughout the school year.

September	**FORM** • Establish goals, norms, and expectations for each member and for the group as a whole • What is everyone hoping to get out of the yearlong study? • What are you doing, and what would you like to do more of?

October	**DEFINE**
	• What does it look like to document learners' learning and work now?
	• What technology are we using now?
	• How can we document process over product?
	• What resources are available to advance learner documentation?
	• Who is our target audience, and what documentation could be used?
	  – Fellow educators (shared assessments)
	  – Learners (portfolio of learning)
	  – Parents (learner process)
	• What learner work should be shared with a larger audience (ethical/legal)? How should learner work be shared? Should learner work be shared?

November	**IDEATE** • How might we use technology to better document learner process over product and document learners' learning? • Use Google Clips, Google Classroom, Seesaw, and 360-degree cameras to collect work in progress and learner reflections. • Create prompts and reminders for learners to reflect on their work in progress, and upload to their Google Classroom to share with the educator as part of a project.
December–March	**DESIGN AND IMPLEMENT** • Using different documentation ideas in lessons and projects with learners • Testing out different ways to document

April	**REFLECT**
	• Collecting data, documentation, and reflections on what worked well, what did not work and why, what we would have done differently, and what we would like to continue to use
	• Produce a presentation and materials to share with the community including samples of the documentation:
	• How was data used in assessment and reflection on lessons and student learning?
	  – How did learners use the tools?
	  – How did we organize the documentation?
	  – How do we plan on continuing to use the documentation tools in the future?
	  – How might other educators consider incorporating the documentation tools in their work?

May	**SHARE** • Present materials and reflections on the work explored this year to the larger school community.

Create, Share, and Grow: Cohort Results

Throughout the school year, educators met, worked individually or with a colleague, shared their ideas, and received feedback. The cohorts included a diverse set of educators from different divisions and departments within the school. The cohorts provided an opportunity for the school library department to advocate and model "respect for diverse perspectives to guide the inquiry process" (AASL 2018, School Librarian III.C.2.). Cohort members engaged in work with learners based on the participants' work within their learning cohorts. Facilitators managed the schedules, shared meeting reminders, kept track of where people were in the process, and shared resources within and among teams. The organization and facilitation of these cohort groups engaged the library staff in "cultivating networks that allow learners to build on their own prior knowledge and create new knowledge" (AASL 2018, School Librarian III.B.2.). Cohort members were examining aspects of their existing curriculum, brainstorming extensions or new resources to use, and engaging with their fellow educators and learners to gain feedback. The professional development cohort experience illustrated the social and shared benefits of learning and experimenting together, highlighting "that learning is a social responsibility" (AASL 2018, School Librarian III.D.2.).

The school library team helped cohort members learn about the makerspace resources in the library for a maker project with a seventh-grade English educator, shared websites and virtual-reality materials for a fourth-grade educator's study of the National Park System, and worked with a fifth-grade educator to develop a digital resource guide for his learners' Ancient Rome research project. One member of our team worked with a group of elementary educators to create a website focused on books that highlighted diversity, equity, and inclusion to share with other educators. Another member of the school library department collaborated with other educators to use iPads and 360-degree cameras to document learners' engagement in collaborative projects and collect learners' reflections on their processes to better understand what learners were learning during collaborative building projects. Finally, a school library department member worked with a fifth-grade educator to design a social-emotional learning project in which learners designed video games to teach younger learners about making decisions responsibly. All these projects illustrate ways the school library staff, through professional development cohorts, were "modeling the use of a variety of communication tools and resources" (AASL 2018, School Librarian III.B.1.) while participating in "department or grade-level curriculum development and assessment" (AASL 2018, School Library III.B.2.). The professional development cohorts were a way for the school library department to better understand the curricular needs of different grade levels and departments, helping us to build the best school library collection and resources to meet the needs of fellow educators and learners, "reinforcing the idea that information is a shared resource" (AASL 2018, School Library III.D.2.).

Connections to AASL Standards

The professional development experience described in this chapter met many AASL Standards related to collaboration in the school library. The professional development cohorts were an opportunity to develop relationships that continue to grow. The cohort-based professional development positioned the school librarian as a leader in the school community who helped educators and learners meet the goals of the whole school and make deeper connections with the school library curriculum. In addition, the learning cohorts opened up dialogue among different groups in the school community, highlighted the social nature of learning, and facilitated social and intellectual learning networks. The groups allowed the school librarians to engage in collaborative planning and to work with other educators, thereby increasing the use of school library spaces and resources. The whole process was inquiry based. The learning cohorts were based on the interests of the educators and the school librarians as well as their work, giving them the time and space to pursue timely and relevant topics and questions that had an immediate and positive impact on the learning environment of learners. With the AASL Standards Framework, school librarians have a blueprint for creating engaging and innovative professional development opportunities. When school librarians embrace the idea of leading and modeling the type of change they want to see, they can use their position in the school community to drive the innovation. In the end, the culture of the school will be more collaborative, resulting in collaborative and engaging learning experiences for learners, preparing them for college, career, and life.

Questions for the Reflective Practitioner

1 What innovative strategies can I use to engage fellow educators in professional development?

2 How can my leadership of school-wide or district-wide professional development result in more collaborative educators and lead to a more collaborative environment for learners?

3 In what ways can I advocate and lead professional development in my school or district to foster a more collaborative professional atmosphere?

2

Moving Beyond Providing Support and Resources

Successful collaborative education is about relationships.
Relationships are an essential part of the teaching process. Research
shows that when educators and learners build strong relationships,
they can improve student achievement, reduce behavioral issues, and
increase learners' motivation (Cassel, 2018). The benefits of relationship-building
also hold true for the educator-to-educator relationship. If school librarians and
other educators want to foster a culture of collaboration, they must build relationships with each other. For school librarians, relationship-building is a critical step if
the goal is to move beyond recommending resources and skills to being co-teachers
and co-designers of learning experiences.

Many school librarians feel isolated at times. In many cases school libraries are
located in spaces in schools—or even in buildings—separate from the classrooms of
learners and educators with whom the school librarians wish to collaborate. School
library time with classes might be scheduled during prep time for classroom educators, resulting in learners being dropped off for their library time and the educator
leaving to do planning or other work. For those starting out in the school library
profession, this autonomy over a curriculum or space can feel wonderful. School
librarians rule their own domains, having opportunities to create curriculum and
design units without needing to work with grade-level partners or departmental
groups. Over the years the isolation can grow, a circumstance that is not optimal
for learners. Learners should be engaging in inquiry-based projects that incorporate information-literacy skills and technology and that have deep connections to
other areas of study. School librarians must continue to grow as lifelong learners,
engaging with other educators to share ideas, improve teaching practices, receive

feedback, and welcome different perspectives. School librarians need to develop relationships with fellow educators and create a professional learning community that results in better integrated learning experiences for student learners and keeps school librarians engaged and a part of the school community.

Developing Relationships for Curricular Connections

The school library plays an essential role in creating an environment of collaborative learning, a foundation that school librarians can use to connect to fellow educators and their curricula. When a school librarian builds relationships with other educators rooted in the subject areas and topics on which learners are focusing in their classrooms, learners have a base of knowledge the school librarian can build upon. In addition, the classroom educators will be more invested in collaboration when they can see benefits to learners in the context of the classroom curriculum.

When the school librarian knows the classroom curriculum and builds relationships with other educators, the school librarian can move beyond providing support and resources for educators to becoming a collaborative partner in instructional design and delivery. These types of partnerships are also in the best interest of learners, helping them to build broader competencies while meeting the subject-area curriculum standards that are set for them.

The AASL Standards call on school librarians to collaborate in their schools by "partnering with other educators to scaffold learning and organize learner groups to broaden and deepen understanding" (AASL 2018, School Library III.A.1.). For that kind of collaboration to happen, school librarians need to know the topics, materials, and subject areas that are being explored in the classroom, as well as the standards and learning outcomes for the classroom, and to establish points of alignment for all of that with the school library curriculum and with school, state, and national standards. School librarians must have conversations and discussions with their collaborating partners about the progress learners have made toward achieving their goals and outcomes, the challenges and struggles that might be happening, and the different learning styles of the learners involved.

When developing and building a collaborative, inquiry-based school library that presents opportunities for learners to explore information literacy in a variety of formats, connecting that inquiry to classroom and subject-area curriculum is essential for learners to have richer and deeper learning experiences. The relationship-building between the school librarian and fellow educators is essential to advancing the learning experiences for learners. When the research and exploration that learners are engaged in have connections to topics and areas of study from other areas of their education, the skills become more concrete for them. It is in the best interest of the learners, the school librarian, and the classroom educators to find opportunities for collaboration and connections in the curriculum. When school librarians and other educators develop strong working relationships, they form deeper connections to the learning goals, helping "the school achieve curricular goals and meet learners' personalized learning needs" (AASL 2018, 89).

When school librarians are able to approach fellow educators from a place of knowledge and understanding of the classroom curriculum, they are likely to be met with appreciation for taking the time to better understand the needs of the learners and the educators. The other educators are more likely to be open to shared teaching experiences if their own curriculum goals are involved. School librarians can stay up to date on the curriculum by attending meetings with grade levels and departments whenever possible to better understand the learning goals and any changes to the subjects or topics being studied in the classroom. Staying informed can happen by making an effort to ask educators about what is happening in their classrooms, offering to seek out resources and materials to support a subject area, or volunteering for curriculum committees. The better informed the school librarian is about the curricula of different grade levels, the more likely it will be to find connections.

START WITH ONE CONNECTION

My path to becoming a collaborative co-teacher with fellow educators started with a good piece of advice from school librarian Todd Burleson. Burleson is the school librarian at the Hubbard Woods School in Winnetka, Illinois. He runs an amazing program and space. When working with other educators and classroom educators in the school, his advice is "just find one!" Just find one educator who is willing to collaborate and design lessons and projects with the school librarian. Build a foundation with that educator and then share the collaborative work and projects with others in the building. Once other educators start to see the benefits of a collaborative partnership with the school librarian, more educators will be open to collaboration. It only takes one to start. Start with one educator and then build a squad, find a crew, and develop more relationships with other educators to build more collaborative partnerships.

The idea of moving to a more collaborative co-teaching environment with other educators can seem daunting at first, and the inclination can be to go all in and try to revamp all library lessons for all learners in all grade levels. However, trying to build collaborative partnerships with every fellow educator in the building simultaneously will be overwhelming for the school librarian—and for other educators, too. The result? A huge sense of failure and defeat when everything doesn't happen at once. Just find one! To start with, just find one classroom educator or grade level to talk to and plan a collaborative project. Focusing on working with one fellow educator will help the school librarian develop a relationship that can grow and advance as they work together and open the door for more collaboration as the work is shared with the larger community.

To begin to make those connections, the school librarian can share book titles at school meetings, run a tutorial on database use, or introduce a new piece of technology, a website, or an app and emphasize some of its connections to a grade-level or classroom curriculum. Create a digital newsletter highlighting materials and services and send it to faculty and staff on a regular schedule. Include offers to collaborate using the materials in a classroom unit or project. Offer to take part in school field trips, committees, or other social opportunities as a way to spend time with and develop relationships with educators. Attend grade-level or departmental curricular meetings to make connections with fellow educators. The hope is that one educator will reach out and the relationship can start to grow.

COLLABORATE IN ACTION: CODING AND STORYTELLING

Sarah Beebe is a technology education teacher. Her schedule is packed with not only teaching technology to grades Pre-K–5 but also managing the devices. This schedule can be overwhelming and busy. Finding time to attend meetings during the school day or to sit down for a planning session can be almost impossible. She was open to collaboration, but finding the time was a challenge. At several after-school faculty meetings, I started sharing the new technology that the school library had acquired, including some new programmable robots. This sharing was a way for me to ensure that I was "promoting and modeling the importance of information-use skills by publicizing to learners, staff, and the community available services and resources" (AASL 2018, School Library III.C.3.). The school library was moving in the direction of using more technology, and this educator wanted to expand the technology education program to the preschool classrooms. However, this expansion was a struggle because preschoolers had no set "technology time." Here was a great opportunity for collaboration between the school librarian and another educator. The preschoolers did have a set time to visit the school library. I wanted to integrate more technology, and Beebe was looking for time to integrate more technology. Here were intersecting goals! Collaboration was the key to both of us helping learners reach our learning goals.

Think: Finding an Intersecting Goal

The discussion and planning of a collaborative project happened over a couple of short meetings and e-mail conversations about what each of our departments wanted to achieve with a collaborative lesson. In the school library, I was working on sequencing in storytelling. I wanted learners to think about the beginning, middle, and end of stories and be able to listen to a book and retell the events of the story in the correct order. This is an important pre-literacy skill that was part of the school library curriculum. The technology education teacher wanted an opportunity to introduce simple coding with learners using the Bee-Bot robot. The device has directional arrow buttons on it; pressing these buttons in the desired sequence, then pressing Go makes the robot move through the programmed series of directions. Here was an opportunity for us to create a shared collaborative lesson that helped each of us accomplish some of our student learning goals.

First, learners in small groups listened to a simple story. Next, they worked with their classmates to recall and talk about the story, learning from each other and organizing their images (photocopies of key illustrations depicting important events) to map out the sequence of the story on the floor in the correct order. Learners then collaborated again within their group to code the Bee-Bot robot to follow the path of the story from beginning to end—and then problem-solve if the Bee-Bot robot did not follow the path learners needed it to follow. The literacy activity integrated with the coding project was a way of "challenging learners to work with others to broaden and deepen understandings" (AASL 2018, School Librarian III.A.1.). The educators had organized "learner groups for decision making and problem solving" (AASL 2018, School Librarian III.A.3.).

The lesson helped preschoolers to work on their pre-literacy skills and introduced them to the basics of coding. This simple lesson was a collaborative experience that helped learners reach both technology education and school library curricular goals. Connections happened because of conversations between two colleagues. The collaborative lesson also became the foundation for a professional relationship that has grown over the past five years and has resulted in in-depth lessons, projects, a collaborative partnership, and, ultimately, a merged school library and technology education department.

In this case, starting with a small lesson began a complete shift in the culture of the school library and the technology education department into an integrated learning department with a foundation in collaboration. Again, just find one! Small projects and one-time lessons can start to lay the foundation for the school librarian to reach a larger, long-term goal of co-teaching and designing learning experiences for learners.

Create and Grow: Innovating to Inspire

A constant phrase heard from classroom educators is, "I can't add one more new thing!" When school librarians seek a collaborative partnership, the best strategy is not to add one more thing to fellow educators' to-do lists but, instead, to see an existing lesson or project as an opportunity for a collaborative and mutually beneficial shared learning experience for the learners. School librarians can see this existing lesson or project as an opportunity to take what they know about the classroom curriculum, find the intersections with the school library curriculum, and present a thoughtful and complete project idea to their fellow educators. By taking on the initial design challenge of the lesson or project, detailing the connections with the classroom curriculum and standards, and seeking feedback and creative input from their fellow educators, the school librarian is removing the biggest challenge to the collaboration. Fellow educators have the opportunity to provide feedback and insight about the flushed-out project, now making the idea of adding "one more new thing" more manageable. The opportunity for fellow educators to offer creative feedback and thoughts about the project idea is another way for school librarians to cultivate "a learning environment that supports and stimulates discussion from all members of the school community" (AASL 2018, School Library III.D.1.) The school librarian has shown that she knows the curriculum, has taken the needs of the classroom educator into account, has provided a creative and engaging project for learners, and is now seeking the input of fellow educators to improve on the idea. It is a win-win scenario for everyone involved!

COLLABORATE IN ACTION:
TECHNOLOGY AND THE MIDDLE AGES

The fifth-grade curriculum was set and packed. The yearlong focus was on perspective; this theme was woven into a curriculum that included literature and reading group studies, as well as the social studies topics of Ancient Rome in the fall and the Middle Ages in the spring. No blocks of time or openings in the schedule would allow for a new project. I was trying to find a way to incorporate more technology, maker empowerment, and collaborative group work into my work with the fifth graders but was running into roadblocks because of the tight schedule. I regularly suggested more in-depth projects during the school library time, but because no direct connection to the packed fifth-grade curriculum existed, the answer was, "We would love to, but we just don't have time for another project." Over the years, the interactions remained the same—collecting books, suggesting websites, and highlighting use of the school library's databases. The key to making a collaboration happen was in my proposing a project that had a deeper connection to one of the longer in-depth social studies units.

Whenever possible, I started attending the fifth-grade curriculum meetings to get a better understanding of the goals for the Middle Ages study. I also paired up with fifth-grade educators at workshops and faculty meetings to hear more about what was happening in the classroom and what goals the team members had for their learners. I learned that the fifth-grade learners had been working on Scratch coding. An AASL Best Website for Teaching and Learning, Scratch is a free online coding program that teaches learners the basics of drag-and-drop coding. With that new information, I started to sketch out the framework for a collaborative learning group project that connected the research that learners did on different roles in medieval society, audio recordings with Scratch programming, and learners' collaborative design and planning of interactive displays.

Create and Share: Co-Planning for Curricular Extensions

I wrote up an outline of the project idea. In the Middle Ages study, each fifth-grade class focuses on a different center of medieval life: castle, market, and cathedral. Each learner is given a job or role that someone in the Middle Ages would have had, researches that role, and makes connections between that position and the larger society. Learners then use their research to make connections with other aspects of the curriculum, including writing and drama. The goal of the project is for learners to develop a better understanding of the interconnected nature of societies and how these different centers of medieval life impacted the lives of citizens. I focused on outlining a project that would use materials and research that learners were applying in their classroom work and, through a collaborative technology project, make connections with the big-picture idea of the interconnectedness of society.

For this collaborative project, each class would plan, design, and build an interactive wall that used Scratch coding, Makey Makey boards, and audio recordings that illustrated life in the different areas of medieval society. The wall would be wired so that when someone touched a button, an audio recording would play, with individual learners talking about their role in medieval society. The wall would be designed to illustrate the different centers of life. Learners would be divided into two groups—a technology planning group and a design group. The technology planning group would be responsible for collecting all the audio recordings from their classmates, wiring the Makey Makey and the board, connecting the wires, coding all the audio files in Scratch, downloading the program to the Raspberry Pi, and connecting the speakers. The design group would be responsible for planning and creating the layout and art for the board to show each location: castle, market, or cathedral. The design group had to make sure the board included pictures representing all the roles that classmates had researched and that the layout and design conveyed life accurately. Each group had to start the process by setting group norms, listing jobs, and deciding who would be responsible for what part of the project. I shared the framework with the classroom educators, making connections to their shared curricular goals:

- Continuation of learner work with maker materials, including Makey Makey and Scratch
- Exploration of multimedia (audio recordings, connecting to coding and computer science), sharing literature and central topic studies for learners to see deeper connections with technology and other subject areas
- Building communication, collaboration, and compromise skills within the committee groups in which learners would be working—they would need to work together to determine the role of each learner and the list of tasks that needed to be accomplished and to keep track of the timeline to ensure that they completed the project on time

- Learner ownership of their work, which would be shared with the larger school community
- Deep connections with STEM (science, technology, engineering, and mathematics) week, incorporating original ideas with the central topic, storytelling, and art, moving toward STEAM (science, technology, engineering, art, and mathematics)

The fifth-grade educators reviewed the plan and offered feedback and connections. As a school librarian, part of "demonstrating how to solicit and respond to feedback from others" (AASL 2018, School Librarian III.C.1.) is being open and responding to feedback provided by other educators. The fifth-grade educators suggested that learners take information from the narratives they had written about their position in medieval life and use that material for the audio recordings as an extension of writing and research they had already done. The educators added time limits for the audio recordings to support the goal of having learners synthesize the most important aspects of their character's role and its place in medieval society. The fifth-grade team liked the connections to Scratch and the idea that this coding skill would be extended to storytelling and amplifying learner voice. They also saw connections to the collaborative group work in which learners would be engaged and to the development of communication and negotiation skills that is fostered in fifth grade.

The project took place at the end of the school year, a perfect time for a project that was a continuation of the learners' medieval study. The project fit into everyone's schedule because it incorporated research and information on which the learners had been focused for several months. The final connection was the public sharing of the interactive walls in the fifth-grade hallway. In past years the learners had shared the medieval project with parents, but this was the first time that learners had an opportunity to share their work with the wider school community. Because I had learned about the curricular goals of the grade level, I was able to make connections between the grade-level and the school library curricula. Relationships with the classroom educators enabled me to present an opportunity for learners that would connect with an already established curriculum and fit into a packed school year schedule. Connections with the fifth-grade team members and their curriculum unlocked a way of "participating in district, building, and department or grade-level curriculum development and assessment on a regular basis" (AASL 2018, School Library III.B.2.).

Think and Share: Being Flexible and Patient

Part of the collaboration process is listening and being willing to give and take. When school librarians are working with other educators, everyone will need to be flexible and open to new ideas and ways of doing things. The AASL Standards call on school librarians to "promote working productively with others to solve problems"

(AASL 2018, 88). The curriculum design process is an inquiry process, an exploration and questioning process that calls on school librarians and co-teachers to dive more deeply into the learning process to design a learning environment that encourages student learner curiosity and creativity and helps to develop mindsets. As they create engaging inquiry experiences for learners that meet both the school library curriculum goals and co-teachers' goals, school librarians must be open to different perspectives and ideas and model being open to feedback and reflection during the inquiry process. The school librarian needs to be a part of "leading inquiry-based learning opportunities that enhance the information, media, visual, and technical literacies of all members of the school community" (AASL 2018, School Library III.A.2.), but that process cannot and should not happen in isolation. Part of being a leader in developing a collaborative environment in the school community and "advocating and modeling respect for diverse perspectives to guide the inquiry process" (AASL 2018, School Librarian III.C.2.) is the school librarian's willingness to be open to diverse perspectives and feedback from co-teachers and other educators.

COLLABORATE IN ACTION: PICTURING COLLABORATION

The fourth-grade literacy curriculum ran like clockwork. Learners did genre studies and had a number of all-class reads that were done throughout the school year. Finding an entry point to incorporate some of the school library technology and maker empowerment goals established for this grade level was a struggle. I was feeling a bit discouraged. I wanted to move beyond pulling genre books and giving booktalks to pursuing a deep-dive project that was more hands-on and collaborative for the learners and for the educators. When one of the fourth-grade educators approached me about using more picture books in her fairy-tale genre study, this was not the huge, reworked project I was looking for, but it was an opening that could lead to something more. We talked about the themes the educator was hoping to highlight in the selected fairy tales, and she was open to the idea of finding stories that were more diverse than just western European. That was the first step, the first year. Though a small step, it was the beginning. I didn't get everything I wanted out of the collaboration, but it started a dialogue.

The next year the fourth-grade educator and I talked about the fairy-tale genre study and what had worked well with the books selected. Then we talked more about the themes the educator was hoping the learners could identify in the stories: family, courage, dreams, fears, prejudice, love, revenge, empathy, and resilience. We redesigned the project by choosing two fairy tales for each theme. Learners read all the books and then worked in pairs to re-read two of the books with similar themes. The fourth graders talked and worked together to identify illustrations and passages in the books that highlighted one of the themes they were learning about. Learners then shared their theme with the whole class and identified the evidence in the text that highlighted that theme. Because the whole class had read all the books, all learners were familiar with the stories and could ask questions and engage in discussions about the themes and the evidence.

Share: Scaffolding Relationships and Learning

This collaboration with the fourth-grade educator was moving forward. The new approach to studying the fairy-tale genre supported her literacy goals in a way that learners found engaging, and I was being seen more as a co-teacher, not simply a gatherer of books. We were having ongoing discussions about the goals and talking about shared language for the lessons. The fourth-grade educator kept me updated on the classroom discussions about the themes, so I knew where the learners were in their study when they came to the school library and could continue the conversation with them. Beyond just the curricular work, the educator and I were building a trusting professional relationship and doing it in a scaffolded way.

By year three the fourth-grade educator was ready to go even further with a more in-depth project. She was open to a technology and maker project. We started talking a month or so before the study began. Again, we discussed what had worked well and what had not the previous year and what we could do to advance learners' learning. Both of us wanted to integrate more tools and visible thinking into the project and have the collaboration between the learners go deeper. We collaborated to create a framework for the project. The project started with the fairy-tale book reading, theme discussion, and learner pair discussion, but instead of just sharing the evidence of the theme in the book, the learners built interactive storyboards to highlight the theme in action. Collaborative learner pairs read the stories again to find evidence of the theme and then worked together to design and build an interactive storyboard that illustrated that theme. The school library had a collection of Little Bits circuits, simple motors, paper circuits, and Makey Makey boards to add lights, motion, and sound to the boards. We also had a supply of cardboard, paints, construction paper, and yarn for learners to build with.

This project allowed learners to make their thinking and understanding visible in a new way. They had to work together with a partner not only to determine the evidence for their book's theme but also to negotiate, plan, design, think about, and rework their project to make a storyboard that illustrated an action element of the theme in the story. The final step was a big share-out of all the projects. Each pair of learners shared their book, the evidence of their theme, and their interactive storyboard. Learners explained to their classmates why they chose the scene to highlight their theme and how they used the interactive maker elements to highlight the theme. As in past years, all the learners had read all the books, so they were familiar with the stories and engaged in discussion about each pair's project. The project was a success and so was the collaboration. I built a relationship with another educator; we shared ideas and goals over the course of several years. We both gave a little and got a little more each year, ultimately building a more in-depth project that met the classroom goals and the school library curriculum goals. Our relationship led to more collaborative projects throughout the school year as we took time, listened, shared, and were open to give and take.

REFLECTING ON TRUST AS A FOUNDATION TO COLLABORATE

Over several years, I have built a trust with fellow educators and now can propose an idea and find them open to collaboration because we know and trust each other and our work. In the Collaborate best practices listed in the AASL Standards, this need for trust is highlighted: "Personal relationships build trust and are more long lasting than purely work relationships" (AASL 2018, 91). Building that trust is key for any school librarian who wants to move from simply providing support to co-teaching.

Questions for the Reflective Practitioner

1. In what ways can I make connections with the curricular goals of my fellow educators?

2. Do I already have a trusting relationship with a classroom educator who might be the "just one" needed to help me start meeting my collaboration goals? How can I reach out to that educator to deepen this relationship?

3. How can making connections with the curricular goals of fellow educators advance my collaboration goals?

4. How might I prioritize relationship-building to advance fellow educators' curricular work in addition to my own?

3

Leading Mission-Based Collaboration

he TED conference started in 1984, growing from Richard Saul Wurman and Harry Marks's observations that technology, entertainment, and design (TED) were becoming intertwined and would have a huge impact on the world ("Our Organization," n.d.). The conference quickly became a must-attend annual event for people in a variety of disciplines. In the early 2000s, TED became a nonprofit organization and expanded its conferences, fellowships, and grant programs. The organization continues to evolve and expand to this day. Through all these evolutions, the mission of TED has remained the same for more than thirty years: to spread ideas.

In many ways a school library is similar to the TED organization. School libraries are places to explore, create, and share ideas. Therefore, school libraries have many branches of service:

- Inspiring learners to explore books for enjoyment
- Offering resources for information gathering
- Teaching a curriculum that meets school library, state, and district standards
- Co-teaching with and supporting other educators in a variety of subject areas
- Providing access to makerspaces, technology, and more

Just like the TED organization, the school library must have a central mission statement that at its core connects all these branches and extends from the mission statement of the school.

Connecting to the Mission of the School

As school librarians explore the AASL Standards and collaborate with other educators, making connections to the school mission is essential, and school librarians need mission statements of their own for their school libraries. A mission statement provides focus to the work of the school library, even as the educational landscape evolves, while highlighting the role of the school librarian in collaboration. Having a central idea that connects everything in the library and the activities it supports aids school librarians in reaching out to the larger community and administration when sharing the work of the school library and communicating its central role in the life of the school. Just like the TED organization, the school library should have a mission statement that clearly states the goals and purpose of the school library and articulates all the collaborative roles that the library plays in the learning environment.

The AASL Standards call for the school library to "consistently [engage] with the school community to ensure that the school library resources, services, and standards align with the school's mission" (AASL 2018, School Library III.B.1.). The school librarian must evaluate the school library's resources and services to ensure that they connect with the larger mission of the school and align with the goals of the community, highlighting to the administration and the larger community that the school library is essential to learners' success. This evaluation is not a once-and-done task. As stakeholders' expectations, technology, and other resources continue to evolve, so, too, must the school library. However, using the school's mission as a lodestar gives the school librarian a clear guide to the direction this evolution should take.

Articulating in newsletters, reports, and conversations how library resources and services connect to the school's mission is an excellent way to advocate for the school library. These connections will resonate with administrators and other educators. They are already comfortable with the language of the mission statement, and most have embraced the concepts on which the mission is focused. The school librarian's explicitly making connections between the library, its services, and the school's mission demonstrates to stakeholders that the librarian shares their values and is poised to meet the school's goals across grade levels and content areas.

If school librarians are to meet the goals of the *National School Library Standards*—and do all they can to help learners develop the Competencies articulated in the Standards—librarians must have a seat at the table when decisions are made. However, school librarians' inclusion in decisions that directly affect learners' success will happen only when administrators and other educators see that the school librarian shares their goals and is working toward outcomes that can best be reached together. Explicitly—and publicly—making connections between the school's mission and the school library's resources and services helps the librarian get that seat at the table and influence decisions that directly affect learners' success in school and beyond.

COLLABORATE IN ACTION:
ON A MISSION FOR A MISSION STATEMENT

The members of the library and the technology education staffs at the Francis W. Parker School recognized an overlap in their curricula and goals as the library world and the technology education world were merging. Staff members set out to design and create an integrated department. The result was the Integrated Learning and Information Sciences (ILIS) department. The goal was to create a collaborative department that incorporated the information-literacy and research goals of the library, the technology goals of the technology education department, and the project-based learning frameworks and the maker empowerment outcomes intertwined with learner inquiry projects. Staff members of the school library department and the technology education department recognized an opportunity to come together and combine departments, creating a framework that would advance learners and make connections with the competencies and skill sets that are essential in the global economy. Collaboration is the element central to inquiry-based learning, project-based learning, and maker empowerment. For learners to grow in these areas, collaboration is needed between educators, learners, and the materials and services offered by the new ILIS department and the classroom curriculum.

Much thought and work went into creating this department to set it up for success. Over the course of a year, the team, which included school librarians, technology educators, and support staff, met for many hours to create a new curriculum for the new ILIS department. Members of the team talked about the skill sets and learning outcomes they wanted for learners as they worked through all the grade levels.

Members of the team looked at the materials and programs offered in the school library that made deeper connections to the themes of collaboration, critical thinking, and innovation. Team members looked at what was working well and what more could be offered. They examined the collection to determine what books and resources were available that would expand the projects and programs in which learners were engaging. They explored how those projects could delve more deeply into the learning outcomes and empower learner voice.

Team members also reviewed available technology to evaluate what was already effective and how coding, robotics, apps, 3-D printing, and emerging technologies could be integrated into projects that would lead to even more learner engagement and empowerment.

By spring the ILIS team members believed they had built a solid framework with the resources that they offered, the programs and services that they were providing, and the materials and technology available. The team also created a growth plan to expand all these offerings. This process raised a bigger question: How could the team communicate to the administration, educators, and the larger community just what ILIS was and how the goals of the department connected to the goals and mission of the school?

To have the impact the ILIS team members wanted to have on the school community through collaboration, they had to be able to express exactly who they were, what their goals were, and how their work would benefit learners and other educators. The ILIS department needed a mission statement that connected to the larger mission and vision of the school. The first step in crafting a mission statement for the ILIS department was to examine the school's mission and vision statements. This portion of the school's mission and vision stood out to the team:

> The Francis W. Parker School educates students to think and act with empathy, courage and clarity as responsible citizens and leaders in a diverse democratic society and global community.

The mission statement is followed by a vision and values statement that lists the mindsets and qualities that the school community wants learners at the school to possess and educators to embrace in their teaching:

- Openness and growth mindset
- Engagement and creativity
- Inclusiveness and dignity
- Responsibility and collaboration
- Character and citizenship

The school's mission statement and these values were the main focus as team members worked to make clear connections between the ILIS department and the goals of the school. ILIS team members wanted to "ensure that the school library resources, services, and standards align with the school's mission" (AASL 2018, School Library III.B.1.) and to highlight the role the department played in meeting the schoolwide goals. Even as the ILIS team members saw connection with their goals of learner inquiry, project-based learning, and innovation, they had to find a way to express those goals in a focused, straightforward mission statement.

Think: Finding True North

The team turned to the Collective Action Toolkit by frog to identify team members' most important goals for learners (frog, n.d.). Frog is a consulting group that uses the design thinking process and thinking routines to help organizations focus their ideas, projects, services, and products. "The Collective Action Toolkit was created to help community leaders bring together groups to solve shared problems and act on them" (frog, n.d.). The routines in the toolkit help groups focus and problem-solve to move forward with an initiative.

The ILIS group used the "Find True North" routine to help focus the different aspects of the school library curriculum and the main ideas of the school's mission statement to find intersections that would demonstrate to the school community just what the ILIS department is and how the department's work connects to the learning goals of the school. This four-phase routine helped scaffold "enactment of learning-group roles to enable the development of new understandings within [the] group" (AASL 2018, School Librarian III.A.2.). This routine was also a step-by-step way to "[organize] learner groups for decision making and problem solving" (AASL 2018, School Librarian III.A.3.) by allowing every team member to have a voice in a thoughtful and organized way that led to agreements on important decisions.

Find True North Routine

The ILIS department at Francis W. Parker School elected to use the "Find True North" routine from the Collective Action Toolkit by frog as a guide for staff members' strategic thinking about the goals they wanted their mission statement to embody. The Collective Action Toolkit is available for download in four languages and is open-source, allowing for adaptation and use by anyone, in any country, via a Creative Commons license. The ILIS team adapted and followed these steps:

1. **State your goals.** Each member of the team states the goals that are most important to the work of the department and writes them on the whiteboard. In our implementation, to help prioritize goals, we next posted the mission and vision statements of the school.

2. **Put a star on your top choices.** Once each person has contributed, ask everyone to put a star next to the top three ideas they feel are most important and best connect the school library and technology curricula.

3. **Discuss the goals not selected.** Look at the statements that received the fewest stars and talk about why they were not ranked higher. Record any new ideas and combine or edit statements as needed to better capture ideas. Cross out ideas the team agrees to let go. When we worked through the process, many ILIS team members felt that some of the ideas could be combined with others. For example, responsible use of information is an essential part of being a citizen, and building skills using different technologies is a component of growth.

4. **Prioritize the goals.** Identify the goal statements with the highest number of stars. Only three or four primary goals should remain. These can be further prioritized as needed. We looked at the final list of the top goals and found that four words were highlighted most often: collaboration, growth, creativity, and citizenship.

By emphasizing collaboration, growth, creativity, and citizenship in the Finding True North process, team members had focused on the deep mindsets that learners must develop to be responsible members of a society. Many of the skills and aspects of the school library and technology education curricula are in pursuit of developing those mindsets. The ILIS team wanted a mission statement that would stand the test of time, no matter what changed in how resources were accessed, information gathered, or technology advanced. The goals and mission of the combined department would be about facilitating learners' building of mindsets that will help them navigate the changing world, no matter the challenges. The four words that were highlighted the most became the foundation for the ILIS mission statement.

Create: Crafting a Mission of Collaboration

Once the team had the foundation for the mission statement, the challenge was writing it. The ILIS department wanted to ensure that its mission statement clearly stated the core goals of the department—no matter what aspect of the curriculum was being taught—and made a deep connection with the goals and mission of the school. The team took the four words that came out of the Finding True North thinking routine and wove them into a mission statement that expressed the goals and focus of the ILIS department and that could be shared with all stakeholders. Over several months the group worked on a shared document, writing, editing, and rewriting the statement. The final version expressed the heart of what the team members do:

> We host collaborative projects that allow students to engage in experiences that encourage creativity, collaboration, and adaptability. We're passionate about building and facilitating these projects to help students and teachers build connections between departments, grade levels, and the community.

The mission statement expressed the mindsets that were essential to develop in learners: creativity, collaboration, and adaptability. All the work that the department does has these mindsets at the center. By making clear connections to the mission of the school and to the goals of other educators in the building, the ILIS department emphasized its role in the learning of the school and its aim of working with others to reach not only the ILIS department's goals but also the goals of the other departments and grade levels in the school. The following goals for learners are implied by this mission statement:

- Learners will be creative thinkers and have the opportunity to express and grow that mindset—creative as readers, exploring all different types of literature; creative in how they gather knowledge; creative in how they express that learning and share it with others.

- Learners will develop a collaborative mindset—collaborative in working with other learners and educators and collaborative in gathering and sharing knowledge.
- Learners will be adaptable and will develop a growth mindset that will enable them to change and grow as technology changes, as their communities change, and as perspectives change; learners will be open to the voices and knowledge of others as they engage as productive citizens.
- Learners will be able to grow throughout the school's learning environment, aided by collaboration between ILIS team members and other educators and between ILIS team members and community members outside the school; further, ILIS team members will make connections with stakeholders, thereby "including the school community in the development of school library policies and procedures" (AASL 2018, School Library III.B.3.).
- Learners will make connections between content-area knowledge gained in multiple disciplines because the ILIS team members, with the benefit of their big-picture view of learning in the school, can be part of the "department or grade-level curriculum development and assessment on a regular basis" (AASL 2018, School Library III.B.2.).

Share: Soliciting Feedback

The next step in the process of developing the mission statement was to bring the draft of the statement to the larger school community. Department staff wanted to "solicit and respond to feedback from others" (AASL 2018, School Librarian III.C.1.) to ensure that the mission statement and the philosophy of the ILIS department resonated with other educators and with administrators. The department wanted to gather the opinions of the larger school community, thereby "advocating and modeling respect for diverse perspectives to guide the inquiry process" (AASL 2018, School Librarian III.C.2.).

The feedback confirmed that the mission statement shared the ideas of the ILIS department in a clear and simple way and helped others to better understand the role that the school library was seeking in the curriculum and in the school. Educators clearly made connections between "building and facilitating these projects to help students and teachers build connections between departments, grade levels, and the community," along with the goals of the ILIS department to make deep connections to the classroom curriculum, and developing projects with cross-discipline and ILIS departmental input. The administration responded favorably to the department's commitment to "allow students to engage in experiences that encourage creativity, collaboration, and adaptability" and saw the connection with the larger school mission statement and with the school's vision and values statement, which emphasize growth, empathy, and openness. Administrators also appreciated the focus on making connections with the "community" and with the school's mission to ensure that learners are "responsible citizens and leaders in a diverse democratic society and global community," achieved, in part, by reaching out to the community outside the school walls.

Because the overall feedback was positive, the ILIS team members felt confident that this final iteration of the mission statement was effective in sharing their beliefs and ideas in a way that applied to the many services the school library provides the learners and also in a way that would stay relevant no matter how the materials or resources change over time.

The feedback also included advice to share the "how" of the mission statement in visuals and explanations of the projects in which the ILIS department engaged and how these projects connected to the learning goals and mission statement. This advice was consistent with the general expectation at the school that educators will reflect on how the school community is living its mission and will provide examples of work and learning that demonstrate the mission in action. Administrators asked the ILIS department staff to reflect on how they are "living the mission" and to share their reflections with other educators and the rest of the school community.

Grow: Living the School Library Mission

The question of how the ILIS department lived its mission became a driving focus in the share-out sessions about materials and resources in the library as well as in communications with educators. ILIS department members reflected on the areas on which they intended to focus their teaching and services—intellectual curiosity, innovation, cultural competency, and growth mindset—to ensure that they were making connections to the mission and goals of the school. The reflection process was a visible way of sharing the connections between the school library and the curricular concerns of other educators. The reflective questions generated also served as an assessment tool for school librarians and fellow educators when measuring learners' growth and identifying the successes and areas for improvement in units and projects. The answers to the questions affected the educators' future modifications to the units and projects to optimize them in support of learners' development of competencies and mindsets.

In addition to making fellow educators aware of the assessment process, asking the classroom educators to reflect at the completion of the unit helps the ILIS team monitor whether they are meeting their own departmental goals. Shared reflection also emphasizes to the school community "that learning is a social responsibility" (AASL 2018, School Librarian III.D.2.). Systematically applying the reflective questions to library resources, technology, and services provides prompts and discussion points for reflecting on the materials used in projects and resources added to the collection, helping to demonstrate and reinforce "the idea that information is a shared resource" (AASL 2018, School Library III.D.2.).

Reflection Questions—Are We Still Headed North?

The ILIS team focused on developing mindsets as their "true north" in the department's collaborative work with learners and educators. The following are reflective questions the team uses with educators at the completion of a project as a lens for continuously assessing projects, resources, and departmental goals. Not all questions will apply to every project.

1. **Intellectual Curiosity**
   a. Where do I allow opportunities for learners to exercise their voice and make choices?
   b. How did I allow for learner inquiry to drive questions?
   c. What resources did learners use in this project that you saw for the first time? What questions did learners ask by themselves?

2. **Innovation**
   a. How did I allow my learners to create something new and contribute to the conversation?
   b. How did I allow my learners to show their learning in a way of their own choice?
   c. What did I do to ensure that I did not get eighteen of the same projects?
   d. How did I allow learners to analyze objects and systems to recognize opportunities for innovation?

3. **Cultural Competency**
   a. How might we witness cultural competency behaviors in learners?
   b. Who can I talk to in the building to help my understanding?

4. **Growth Mindset**
   a. How might we allow for positive failure and opportunities for multiple iterations?
   b. How might we encourage learners to keep working when faced with a roadblock?

In summary, engaging in the process of examining the services and resources of the ILIS department, making connections to the school mission, creating an ILIS department mission statement, soliciting feedback, and creating and using reflective questions that look at the work of the school library served several purposes.

- The process ensured that the school library team took a deep look at what they were offering to the learning community—not only the materials and resources but also the projects and units in which learners were engaged—to make sure these experiences connected to the mission and goals of the school community.

- Creating a school library mission statement forced the team to really think about who they were and what they were offering and, in a clear and concise way, to articulate their core purpose in the school.

- Asking for feedback from other members of the school engaged the community in the role and function of the school library. This process confirmed that ILIS's core beliefs matched those of the larger community and were communicated in the best way.
- Creating reflection questions that connect to the school mission and the ILIS mission gave the ILIS team an assessment tool that helps them to
  - better meet their goals,
  - enable learners to engage in experiences that can best help them develop mindsets essential to their learning and meeting of curricular goals, and
  - play a central role in the assessment process.

COLLABORATE IN ACTION: AUTISM MISSION INSPIRES PARTNERSHIP

Teresa Lansford is a school librarian at Lincoln Elementary School in Norman, Oklahoma. Her school library serves three hundred learners; part of the school's mission is to serve differently abled learners in its Autism and Developmentally Delayed Program. Working with learners with autism was a new experience for Lansford when she joined the school community. She was not sure how to best serve those members of her community, so this school librarian started researching and learning more about library services for people with autism. Through her research, she realized that many of the recommendations for story times with children with autism sounded a lot like a program that was run by a librarian at a local public library—a program that used music, repetition, and manipulatives, all recommendations for school library programs for learners with autism. The school librarian decided to reach out to the public librarian to see if she would be willing to model a sensory story time at the school library. The public librarian agreed, enabling the school librarian to observe and learn. She said, "My students' reaction to the public librarian's story time was amazing to watch and framed how I set up my own lessons for years to come." This school librarian's "[facilitation of] diverse social and intellectual learner networks" (AASL 2018, School Library III.C.1.) had her reaching beyond the school building and making connections with the public library that would lead to a long-term collaborative partnership.

After the initial observation and sharing, Lansford saw an opportunity for a deeper collaborative partnership with the public library that would benefit the learners at Lincoln Elementary School and the patrons of the public library. The school had partnered with the public library in the past for family reading night and for coding lessons with the public library's computer center director. Collaboration on a sensory story time was a perfect opportunity to further the relationship and help meet the needs of both the school and public library as the staff sought ways to make deeper connections with the schools to expand public library services and outreach in the community. The school librarian would be able to use the public library's sensory story time resources and collaborate with the public librarians. With this collaboration, Lansford was "reinforcing the idea that information is a shared resource" (AASL 2018, School Library III.D.2.) and, as she said, "I know the power that comes when more people are working together to help learners." This collaboration was a way for both libraries to meet their mission and goals to serve all members of the school and larger community.

Think and Create: Co-Planning and Sharing Resources

The school librarian and the public librarian began meeting to plan sensory story times. They planned to host sensory story times for the learners at Norman Elementary School, with the school librarian hosting library lessons for learners and then the public librarian coming to the school once a month to supplement the sensory story time lessons. They met face to face to design the lessons, and the public librarian observed the school librarian's lessons so that the public librarian could structure her story times with the same framework. The sensory story times were all based on research and best practices for learners with autism. To make the transition easy for learners, the two librarians wanted all the sensory story times to have a similar format no matter who was leading. The sensory story time always starts with a song and movement activity, followed by an opening statement to introduce the concept for the story time, such as hot/cold, land/water animals, and the like. Next is a story with manipulatives to aid comprehension and retelling, followed by song and sensory activities related to the content and a sharing of more sensory manipulatives. The transition to each new activity is a song and movement activity. The story time ends with a closing song. The public librarian brings the sensory manipulatives for the lessons because the public library has a large supply of resources that help to supplement the resources at the school library.

The two librarians follow Norman Elementary School's curriculum map so that the sensory story times are anchored in themes and concepts that the learners are covering in their classrooms. This collaboration highlights how the school library and the public library can "scaffold learning and organize learner groups to broaden and deepen understanding" (AASL 2018, School Library III.A.1.) by designing and creating a sensory story time that engages learners with autism while making connections with the curriculum of the school and meeting goals of both libraries.

Through distributing flyers at the school and posting information on the school library's Facebook page, the public librarian can share information about additional programming and resources available at the public library with the families of the learners with autism. The communications to the community were a way to "consistently [engage] with the school community to ensure that the school library resources, services, and standards align with the school's mission" (AASL 2018, School Library III.B.1.) by sharing resources and services from the public library to better serve the learners at the school.

Share and Grow: Spreading the Collaboration

The partnership and collaboration between the school and public librarians have been a great success for the school and especially for the learners with autism. The school librarian shared the program, lessons, and resource ideas at district-wide school librarian meetings and with school librarians outside the district whom she knew also worked with learners with autism. By sharing with other school librarians, Lansford was able to expand the impact of the program to benefit more learners. She "[promoted] and [modeled] the importance of information-use skills by publicizing to learners, staff, and the community available services and resources; serving on school and district-wide committees; and engaging in community and professional activities" (AASL 2018, School Library III.C.3.). The district director of media services and instructional technology also shared information about the program with other librarians through meetings and e-mail communications. Lansford was named the District Teacher of the Year, further widening the audience to administrators and principals who were able to learn about the collaboration and program. The success of the sensory story time program has continued to grow, and the two librarians had an opportunity to co-present at the Oklahoma Library Association Conference, spreading the impact of the program to benefit more learners with autism in more districts. The school librarian's outreach about her program "[demonstrates] and [reinforces] the idea that information is a shared resource" (AASL 2018, School Library III.D.2.). By sharing the design of the program throughout the district and state, the school librarian "[designed] and [led] professional-development opportunities that reinforce the impact of the school library's resources, services, and programming on learners' academic learning and educators' effectiveness" (AASL 2018, School Library III.C.2.).

Reflecting on this program, Lansford advises other school librarians hoping to develop collaborative partnerships with the public library "to find a need and start a dialogue. As teachers we want kids reading; we want families using the public library. We all win when we team up." She also recommends that school librarians stay active in local organizations as a way to meet other librarians, allowing school librarians to learn more about the public library program and see goals and outcomes that reflect the school's mission and values. Making these connections is a way of "creating and maintaining a learning environment that supports and stimulates discussion from all members of the school community" (AASL 2018, School Library III.D.1.). This school librarian goes on to say, "It never hurts to ask. You never know when someone may be looking for an opportunity to do outreach and may not even realize opportunities exist." The collaboration process always starts with a conversation. "Don't wait for others to come to you. As collaborators and co-teachers, school librarians see the value of partnerships on a daily basis. Share the power with others."

Through this collaborative program, a school librarian ensured that her school library met the mission and goals of her school, which include providing a learning environment in which learners with autism can be successful and advance in their learning. The collaborative relationship with the public librarian resulted in "creating and maintaining a learning environment that supports and stimulates discussion from all members of the school community" (AASL 2018, School Library III.D.1.) and the public library that resulted in so many benefits for the school librarian's learners. School librarians must be open to unique collaborative relationships that extend beyond the school community and fellow educators to ensure that the school library maximizes its impact on learning by making connections to the mission and goals of the school.

Questions for the Reflective Practitioner

1. In what ways is my school library making clear connections to the mission of the school? How might I collaborate with others in the school community or outside the community to develop deeper connections?

2. How might I, my district's school library department, or the district library develop a mission statement or reflection process that ensures that the school library curriculum is meeting the mission of the school?

3. In what process, professional development, or thinking routines could I engage with fellow school librarians and educators in my school and beyond to develop a clear mission statement and process to ensure that everyone is working toward shared goals for learners and the school community?

PART II

Student Learners as Mindful Collaborators

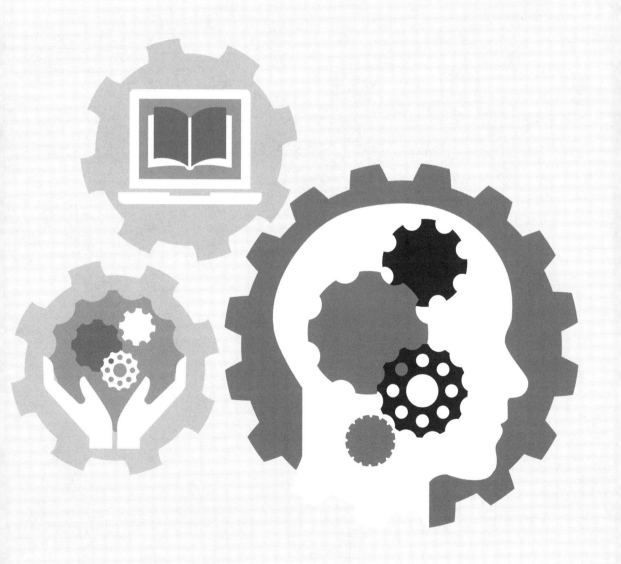

4

Developing the Collaboration Mindset in Learners

n its "Future of Jobs Report," the World Economic Forum released a list of the skills that individuals will need to be successful in the changing world. By the year 2020, some of the skills that employers will be looking for include cognitive flexibility, negotiation skills, a service orientation, emotional intelligence, and the ability to coordinate with others (Curtin 2018). Collaboration is the foundation of all these skills.

- *Cognitive flexibility* is the ability to adapt how individuals communicate based on who they are talking to. Offering learners collaborative opportunities in which they talk to different groups, hear various perspectives, and can practice adapting to these different voices and perspectives is essential to developing this skill.

- *Negotiation skills* are part of being able to listen to the needs of others, think about those needs, and compromise to reach an agreement that benefits all. Collaboration and group work must include listening, sharing, and negotiating with others to reach common goals.

- When people are *service oriented*, they are thinking about how they can help others. Collaboration requires individuals to think about and help others, not just themselves.

- *Emotional intelligence* is the ability of individuals to read others' reactions to them and to understand their impact on others. High emotional intelligence is key to successful collaboration because collaborators need to listen to and compromise with others, and better understanding of others and of oneself is essential to achieving compromise.

45

- *Coordinating with others* is all about collaboration, adjusting to others, and being open to different perspectives and voices.

Collaboration is at the center of these skills and mindsets. Educators must focus on developing a collaborative mindset in learners to help prepare them for the world so that they can actively participate as citizens.

The AASL Standards call for learners to "work effectively with others to broaden perspectives and work toward common goals" (AASL 2018, 85). Developing this skill in learners must go beyond group work and delve deeply into the idea of working effectively with others by focusing on listening and incorporating perspectives toward shared and common goals. Learners need to be given opportunities to work with others, compromise and negotiate, fail, then rethink their plans. When learners have opportunities to work through the collaborative process, they develop the skills to share knowledge, listen to feedback, and find solutions to problems. Relationships and connections that learners nurture through collaborative opportunities are essential for them to understand that learning is a social responsibility and that they cannot grow as learners in isolation. Collaboration is a skill and a mindset that must be cultivated in learners throughout their education and must be at the core of learners' experiences so that the skill becomes engrained and learners will use it outside school. The world is changing at a rapid rate. Educators must be part of helping learners develop the skills and mindsets that they will need to be engaged citizens and workers in a global society.

Developing Mindsets through the Domains

The AASL Shared Foundations—Inquire, Include, Collaborate, Curate, Explore, and Engage—represent the core values that lifelong learners should reflect on and cultivate as they prepare for college, career, and life. The Domains—Think, Create, Share, and Grow—describe the continuum that learners move through as they engage in learning, gaining competency in the Shared Foundations (AASL 2018, 15–17). Just as multiple Shared Foundations can be present within a single project or lesson, learners can engage in several Domains at once and can enter and re-enter the process at different points. The learning process can look different depending on the developmental stage of the learner. The Domains are an essential part of the AASL Standards, not just to integrate the Competencies but to understand where learners are in their development and to better document and determine the learning process. The Domains remind school librarians to focus on the learner when developing mindsets in learners and to think about the process more than the product. The Domains provide educators a progressive but flexible structure to integrate the skills outlined in the Learner Competencies while developing those deeper mindsets present in the Shared Foundations and Domains. These mindsets are essential to learners' ability to adapt to the ever-changing world. The communication tools that learners use will always be changing as technology evolves and society adapts, but developing and maintaining a creative mindset is a constant no matter the medium. The ways in which learners interact with groups can be in flux as our global society becomes more interconnected, but being a critical thinker is a mindset that is eternally essential to being a productive citizen. As school librarians design and develop learning experiences, the Competencies are the elements that may evolve as our world evolves, but the Domains are a fundamental constant to cultivating mindsets in learners.

This chapter recognizes the nonlinear characteristics of the Domains while examining the learning outcomes unique to each Domain. Each Domain and the mindset cultivated through its implementation are explored in-depth through unit projects and learners' experience. In this chapter, each "Collaborate in Action" example will illustrate and concentrate on the qualities developed through a specific Domain, though examples may at times stray into other Domains because that is the nature of learning. The chapter concludes with a unit that develops the Collaborate mindset while showcasing the nonlinear characteristics using all the Domains in concert. Through this chapter, readers will recognize the individual nature of the Domains as well as the interconnectedness that exists in cultivating the mindset of Collaborate in learners.

THINK MINDSET

The Think Domain prompts learners to "inquire, think critically, and gain knowledge (AASL 2018, 15). Under the Learner Competencies for Collaborate, the Think Domain empowers learners to make connections with knowledge and expand their understandings while recognizing that the perspectives and understandings of their fellow learners are an essential component of their own inquiry and learning. Learners must develop the ability to listen to others, make connections with previous knowledge, seek new knowledge, and work with fellow learners to define and solve problems. When examining the Think Domain in developing the Collaborate mindset in learners, school librarians need to focus on engaging learners in experiences whereby learners share knowledge and understandings with each other in developing new knowledge.

Collaborate in Action: Storytelling and Biography

One area of study in the second-grade curriculum that I focus on is biography. Learners in small groups read multiple biographies with educators and engage in conversations about the lives of individuals and how they were change makers in their fields of study, in their communities, or in the world. The goal of this project is for learners to "broaden and deepen [their] understandings" (AASL 2018, Learner III.A.1.) through the exploration of biographies of individuals they might not be familiar with and to "[develop] new understandings through engagement in a learning group" (AASL 2018, Learner III.A.2.). The exploration of these biographies takes place in whole-class groups or in small groups in which learners discuss and make their own connections with other learners' reflections and connections. One of these projects, a collaboration with the technology education teacher, was an in-depth look at a biography of Harriet Powers combined with a maker project in which learners would "[decide] to solve problems informed by group interaction" (AASL 2018, Learner III.A.3.). The weekslong project allowed learners to make deep connections to the information they were studying and to incorporate primary source materials and engaged learners in a design and maker project that made their thinking and understanding visible.

Deepening Understanding in a Collaborative Group

To begin, the book *Sewing Stories: Harriet Powers' Journey from Slave to Artist* by Barbara Herkert was read aloud to the whole class. The book tells the story of Harriet Powers, who was born into enslavement in Georgia. As a young child she learned the art of quilt making from her mother and other women in her community. Powers learned how to stitch, dye fabrics, and design quilt squares to tell stories. After the end of slavery in the United States, Powers, her husband, and children ran a small farm, and she continued to make quilts. When the family fell on hard times during a drought and were not able to make enough money selling produce from their farm, Powers sold her quilts to support the family. She went on to share her work at craft exhibitions, and her work was commissioned by organizations in and around Atlanta, Georgia. Powers's work is considered some of the best examples of Southern Folk Quilt art. Two of her pieces have survived and are now on display at museums, one at the Boston Museum of Fine Arts and one at the Smithsonian. As the second graders listened to the story, they engaged in collaborative discussions about Powers's life, asked deep questions about her experiences, and made connections with other biographies they had heard and read, including books about Harriet Tubman and Sojourner Truth. This process demonstrated learners' "desire to broaden and deepen [their] understandings" (AASL 2018, Learner III.A.1.) of a different time period, learning about someone else's experiences while making deep connections to prior knowledge.

Using Primary Sources, Thinking Routines, and Engagement in a Learning Group

The next step was to study Harriet Powers's work. We explained to learners the definition of primary source materials—that they are original materials, journals, articles, and art from the actual time period or event. Learners explored Powers's two quilts that are in museums. The educator team printed pictures of the quilt squares from the museums' websites and hung them on a whiteboard wall so that learners could explore them in a gallery-type setting. The goal was for learners to explore the quilt squares to better understand the idea of using images to tell stories, as Powers and other quilt makers did in their quilt designs. Learners used the thinking routine See/Think/Wonder to explore the squares and share their ideas about what stories Powers was telling with her art. The See/Think/Wonder thinking routine is a tool to broaden and deepen learners' understanding, help them develop new understandings through engagement in a learning group, and identify problems they want to solve as a group. This thinking routine "encourages students to make careful observations and thoughtful interpretations. It helps stimulate curiosity and sets the stage for inquiry" (Harvard Project Zero, n.d.).

See/Think/Wonder Routine

A routine for exploration, the See/Think/Wonder routine from Harvard Project Zero stimulates curiosity and encourages learners to make careful observations and thoughtful interpretations related to their topic of study. This thinking routine asks learners three questions:

1. What do you see?
2. What do you think about that?
3. What does it make you wonder?

Source: Harvard Project Zero, n.d., "See Think Wonder," Visible Thinking.

Learners moved about the library studying images of the quilt squares and, on the whiteboard walls beneath the images, writing what they identified in the squares. Learners considered what concrete connections they could make with the images, what they knew about Powers's life, what they wondered, and what questions they had about the images. Learners continued moving around the room, adding their reflections and making connections to and extensions from the ideas their classmates shared. Using this process, learners "[developed] new understandings through engagement in a learning group" (AASL 2018, Learner III.A.2.). The class came back together to discuss their ideas and reflections and to explore the museum websites to better understand the stories Powers had shared through her artwork. After learners better understood the events and ideas that Powers was telling about in her work, they went back to the quilt squares and identified images that supported the stories and events. This process, again, supported the idea of gaining new knowledge and rethinking and expanding the learners' understanding of the information and research they were collecting.

Making Understanding and Knowledge Visible

After the research and information stage, learners were challenged to make their understanding and knowledge visible by making a quilt that told a story in the style of Harriet Powers's work. Working together as a group, learners brainstormed different experiences from their second-grade year. A list was created of all the memories that learners had of field trips, topics they studied, books they read, and events throughout the year. Then, each learner chose a memory from the school year to share in a quilt square. Next, learners were shown how to use the Google Suite app Google Drawing. The application allows users to draw freehand lines or insert standard shapes. The second graders were shown how to use the Shapes option to design images in the style of Harriet Powers's work. Learners thought about the school year event and how different shapes could be used to create images to tell the story of the experience.

After learners designed their images, the files were saved as .svg files, and the library's makerspace Cricut cutter and these files were used to cut all the images out of fabric. Learners then sewed their fabric images onto quilt squares, and the squares were sewn together to make a collaborative class quilt that told the story of the learners' second-grade year. By telling and sharing their own stories on quilt squares, learners created new knowledge and illustrated their understanding of Harriet Powers's work and the art of telling stories through quilting and images. Learners also mastered new skills, including using Google Drawing to express knowledge and working with fabric and sewing arts as a form of storytelling.

CREATE MINDSET

The Create Domain highlights the need for learners to be able to "draw conclusions, make informed decisions, apply knowledge to new situations, and create new knowledge" (AASL 2018, 15). Through the lens of Collaborate, the Create Domain calls on learners to utilize different communication tools and resources to expand their knowledge and understanding. The Create Domain also calls for learners to collaborate with other learners to expand their own understanding and build new knowledge. Collaborate in the Create Domain recognizes learning as a social activity. Learners must not only gather understanding and knowledge from resources but also talk and listen to other learners to deepen their understanding. In order for learners to work with each other to "create new knowledge," they must be open to different perspectives and ideas.

Collaborate in Action: The Design Thinking Process

Fifth-grade educator Mike McPharlin wanted his learners to develop a deep understanding of the social-emotional concepts they were studying in their curriculum. This educator wanted his learners to think more deeply about responsible decision making, one of the tenets of the social-emotional learning curriculum. McPharlin, technology education teacher Sarah Beebe, and I collaborated to plan a design thinking project that provided a framework for learners to take ownership of the process. Our team also wanted learners to be able to demonstrate responsible decision making, not just define it. The design thinking process has been used for decades in business and product design. In the past few years, it has moved into education as a way to rethink school spaces, schedules, and curricula. In education, design thinking can also be used within lessons and projects as a way for learners to better understand a subject area and to problem solve. David Kelley, the founder of IDEO and the Stanford d.school, said this about the design thinking process: "Design thinking utilizes elements from the designer's toolkit like empathy and experimentation to arrive at innovative solutions. By using design thinking, you make decisions based on what future customers really want instead of relying only on historical data or making risky bets based on instinct instead of evidence" ("Design Thinking" 2019). The design thinking process in the business model has designers focus on the user, including interviews and observations, to ensure that they are really designing a product or experience that the end user will benefit from. The process guides the designer through five steps: empathize, define, ideate, prototype, and test (figure 4.1).

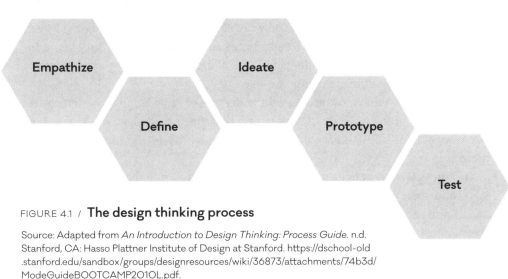

FIGURE 4.1 / **The design thinking process**

Source: Adapted from *An Introduction to Design Thinking: Process Guide.* n.d. Stanford, CA: Hasso Plattner Institute of Design at Stanford. https://dschool-old .stanford.edu/sandbox/groups/designresources/wiki/36873/attachments/74b3d/ ModeGuideBOOTCAMP2010L.pdf.

Our team of educators came up with the idea of having learners design games that teach others how to be responsible decision makers. McPharlin reflected that "if fifth graders could create a game that taught someone else about responsible decision making, that would really show me that they understood the concept themselves." The design thinking process was the foundation of this project because, at its core, the design thinking process is collaborative. To work through the process, learners must communicate with, discuss with, and listen to others and "[establish] connections with other learners to build on their own prior knowledge" (AASL 2018, Learner III.B.2.).

However, before the learners could design games to teach others to be responsible decision makers, the learners needed experience with the design process in an easy and relatively brief project: The Ice-Cream Sundae Design Challenge. The ice-cream sundae design challenge uses the design thinking process to design a perfect sundae for someone else.

Step 1: Empathize

"Empathy is the centerpiece of a human-centered design process. The Empathize mode is the work you do to understand people, within the context of your design challenge. It is your effort to understand the way they do things and why, their physical and emotional needs, how they think about [the] world, and what is meaningful to them" (*An Introduction to Design Thinking,* n.d.).

Applied to education, learners had to be able to conduct an empathy interview and be active listeners to "[establish] connections with other learners" and then translate the information they collected to "create new knowledge" (AASL 2018, Learner III.B.2.). The team wanted the learners to spend the most time in the empathy stage to create a solid foundation on which to work and to become better listeners and better collaborators when it came time to design their games. The classroom educator said, "I wanted my students to develop the ability not only to listen but to listen to design something for someone else."

Being active listeners, observers, and collectors of knowledge to better understand the true problem so that learners can take that knowledge and "create new knowledge" (AASL 2018, Learner III.B.2.) is essential inside and outside the classroom.

To help learners practice the skills needed to be active listeners, information gatherers, and observers, each person participating in the ice-cream sundae challenge interviews a classmate, asking deep-dive questions about some of that individual's favorite memories about food. Learners ask what was the best meal their classmate ever ate. What was the occasion? Who was there? The interviewer asks about a time the interviewee made a dessert. What was it? Why did the classmate choose to make it? Who was there with the classmate? The idea behind these questions is to dive more deeply into the experience and the people the interviewee was with during eating and food experiences to connect on an emotional level. The challenge is that the interviewer has to really listen to what the other person is saying. The process is not just a simple question of what kind of ice cream the interviewees like. The goal is to encourage learners to dive more deeply into information and then be able to process that information and create something new with that knowledge: a unique and personal ice-cream sundae for another person.

Ice-Cream Sundae Design Challenge Empathy Interview

Goal: To gain a better understanding of your interviewee's taste in desserts and better design an ice-cream sundae for that person.

Guiding Questions:

1. What is one of your favorite memories involving a food? Who was there? What made it special? What did you like about it?
2. Tell me about your best meal ever. Who was there? What did you eat? What made it your best meal?
3. What is your favorite memory of making a dessert? What was it? Who else was there?
4. What is a meal you could eat every day for the rest of your life?
5. Do you have any food allergies?

Learners recorded the interviews so that interviewees could speak at their own pace and the interviewers could really focus on listening to the details of the conversation without the distraction of trying to jot down all the information. Learners could give interviewees undivided attention, connecting with the interviewees, and ask follow-up questions to dive deeply into this topic of the interviewee's dessert preferences.

Step 2: Define

"The Define mode of the design process is all about bringing clarity and focus to the design space. It is your chance, and responsibility, as a design thinker, to define the challenge you are taking on, based on what you have learned about your user and about the context. After becoming an instant-expert on the subject and gaining invaluable empathy for the person you are designing for, this stage is about making sense of the widespread information you have gathered" (*An Introduction to Design Thinking,* n.d.). After the fifth graders conducted their interviews, they listened to their interviews several times to make sure they had collected all the data and details they needed. The learners defined the themes and connections they extracted from the interviews. Learners highlighted words from the interviews, writing the words on paper. Next, learners organized the different food words highlighted by the interviewee into categories including salty or sweet, fruit, vegetables, textures, whether they were connected to a particular holiday, and so on. The different categories that learners collected were the foundations they would use to build the ice-cream sundaes.

Step 3: Ideate

"Ideate is the mode of the design process in which you concentrate on idea generation. Mentally it represents a process of 'going wide' in terms of concepts and outcomes. Ideation provides both the fuel and also the source material for building prototypes and getting innovative solutions into the hands of your users" (*An Introduction to Design Thinking*, n.d.). Learners were next given the challenge of taking the information gleaned from the interviews and really thinking about and processing what they had learned about their subject and that person's positive experiences with and memories about food. Using this information, each learner would create a plan for what might be the perfect ice-cream sundae to suit the interviewee's preferences.

Step 4: Prototype

"The Prototype mode is the iterative generation of artifacts intended to answer questions that get you closer to your final solution" (*An Introduction to Design Thinking*, n.d.). Having gathered information about the interviewees' preferences, the fifth graders were ready to build the ice-cream sundae prototypes. The learners were given a wide variety of foods to design their sundaes—some traditional, such as chocolate sauce, sprinkles, and graham crackers, and some nontraditional options, including potato chips, spicy chili sauce, and popcorn. Each learner then built the ideal sundae for the classmate who had been interviewed. Learners shared the ice-cream sundae prototypes they built for their interviewees, giving the interviewees time to eat their ice-cream sundaes and think about the flavor combinations. When each interviewee was done eating, the learners shared the explanation of why they chose the flavors they did and how those choices connected to the information learned from the interviews.

Step 5: Test

> The Test mode is when you solicit feedback, about the prototypes you have created, from your users and have another opportunity to gain empathy for the people you are designing for. Testing is another opportunity to understand your user, but unlike your initial empathy mode, you have now likely done more framing of the problem and created prototypes to test. Both these things tend to focus the interaction with users, but don't reduce your "testing" work to asking whether or not people like your solution. Instead, continue to ask "Why?", and focus on what you can learn about the person and the problem as well as your potential solutions. (*An Introduction to Design Thinking*, n.d.)

After the fifth graders ate their custom-made sundaes, they gave feedback to the designers, sharing what they liked about the dessert and why. The recipients of the sundaes also told the designers what flavors they wished were in the sundae. This sharing was a way for learners to hear authentic feedback from their peers about what they had created. The class gathered to reflect on the empathy interview process and share what they had learned.

Listening as an Essential Tool in the Create Domain

Throughout the ice-cream sundae design process, learners used "a variety of communication tools and resources" (AASL 2018, Learner III.B.1.). They conducted and recorded personal interviews, designed plans for their sundaes, and even used food to illustrate their knowledge and understanding of another learner and to create new knowledge.

When learners develop their communication and active-listening skills, they are able to participate in personal, social, and intellectual networks, use various communication skills, and establish connections with other learners. When learners possess the skills to be active listeners and to collect knowledge, and when they are open to listening to others and hearing various perspectives, they can draw conclusions and make decisions that are more informed. Active listeners are also more likely to be able to achieve the deep understandings that are needed to create new knowledge. The AASL Standards state, "In our increasingly diverse society, effective communication is essential to productive collaboration" (AASL 2018, 86). Being able to ask deep questions, to listen, to process the information and then to apply that information to make or create new knowledge is essential for participation in a global society.

Reflecting on the empathy interview process, the fifth-grade classroom educator stated, "This process really focused on my students developing the skill of listening to truly hear where someone else was coming from and then creating something based on that knowledge." By helping learners develop their listening and communication skills through the empathy interview and the design thinking processes, learners begin to develop the skills that are important "to productive collaboration" (AASL 2018, 86).

After learners went through the ice-cream sundae design challenge process, they were ready to work through the design thinking process in small groups to create games to teach others about responsible decision making. The fifth graders had the communication tools to engage in the interview process with other members of the community, to listen to and share with their group members, and then to take their data and ideas and design a prototype of a game to share with the community and receive feedback. The empathy interview process helped prepare learners to more deeply engage in the Create Domain Learner Competencies, including "establishing connections with other learners to build on their own prior knowledge and create new knowledge" (AASL 2018, Learner III.B.2.). Learners refined their listening skills and better understood how to create with other learners in a collaborative learning environment.

SHARE MINDSET

The Share Domain focuses on learners' abilities to "share knowledge and participate ethically and productively as members of our democratic society" (AASL 2018, 15). When viewing collaboration through the Share Domain, the focus is on learners' development of the ability to "work productively with others to solve problems" (AASL 2018, 36). This ability includes being open to receiving feedback and giving constructive feedback to other learners. The Share Domain also focuses on the need for learners to "[involve] diverse perspectives in their own inquiry processes" (AASL 2018, Learner III.C.2.). Learners need to be open to the voices of others to build more understanding and knowledge. Collaborate under the Share Domain is about learners' ability to be open to other ideas and perspectives in order to solve problems and create new knowledge.

Collaborate in Action: Global Health Challenge

Marcia Buckley is a high school librarian for Harford County Public Schools in Maryland. She engaged in a collaborative project with her school's public health educators and the school librarian from another district high school to provide her eleventh-grade learners with the opportunity to share their work and receive authentic feedback. As part of the public health curriculum, high school learners must create a proposal for the World Health Organization to advocate for more funding to improve public health standards in a developing nation. Learners research the geography, climate, cultural customs, water availability, population, politics, and travel requirements or concerns of a chosen country and then create an informed proposal that articulates the need for public health improvements and how the funds would be used.

The school librarian worked with learners as they accessed authoritative resources and materials in the school library and online to write their proposals. Learners used print materials, online databases, and websites to collect information to inform their writing. The school librarian also focused on providing a wide variety of resources and materials to ensure that learners were "involving diverse perspectives in their own inquiry processes" (AASL 2018, Learner III.C.2.). Learners were provided a rubric for the presentation detailing the information they would need to include in the proposal. In the public health classes, learners were continuing to explore what conditions were essential for people to have healthy communities to ensure that learners understood all the information they would need to create a complete and accurate proposal. At another high school in the district, learners were working through the same process in their public health classes and were working with their school librarian to research and write a proposal for the World Health Organization using the same presentation rubric.

Presentation and Feedback from Peers

After the proposals had been researched and written, each eleventh grader created a presentation to share the research and advocate for the country that would receive the (imaginary) funds. The audience for the presentations was the learners' whole class. All members of each class were expected to provide constructive feedback to their peers about their presentations. For this purpose, learners were given a reflection sheet and were asked to "work productively with others to solve problems by soliciting and responding to feedback from others" (AASL 2018, Learner III.C.1.). Each learner reflected on each classmate's presentation using the Praise, Polish, Question method: articulating something the learner did well, identifying something that needed improvement, and asking a question about the information. Learners were asked to explain their feedback and provide evidence for their comments. All members of each class were also asked to reflect on the overall presentation and to indicate whether they would give this country the funding. Before moving on to the next stage of the project, the learners in each class then chose the five proposals they believed made the best argument and provided the most evidence that the countries needed the public health funding.

Connecting with Another High School to Provide Authentic Feedback

The five proposals from each class that the learners determined were the most deserving of the public health funds were then shared with learners at another high school in the district where learners had engaged in the same process (using the same rubric) in public health class and the school library. After the exchange of proposals, the next step at both schools was for learners to read the selected proposals and provide authentic feedback to the learners at the other school about their work. Learners again engaged in the Praise, Polish, and Question process and provided evidence to determine which of the proposals from the neighboring school made the best evidence-based argument for their countries to receive public health funding.

Learners provided thoughtful feedback and reflection about the projects based on the shared criteria and agreed on the proposals that would be chosen to receive the funding. This project highlighted the connections that school librarians can make across a district curriculum to offer learners opportunities to give and receive authentic "feedback from others" (AASL 2018, Learner III.C.1.) and "[involve] diverse perspectives in their own inquiry processes" (AASL 2018, Learner III.C.2.) by gaining feedback from peers and learners outside their classroom.

GROW MINDSET

The Grow Domain encourages learners to "pursue personal and aesthetic growth" (AASL 2018, 15). The goal of the Grow Domain is for learners to develop the mindset of lifelong learners, to follow the inquiry process, to advance and build their understanding and knowledge. Looking at the Grow Domain through the lens of Collaborate, the focus is on learners "recognizing learning as a social responsibility" (AASL 2018, Learner III.D.2.). Collaboration is about listening to others, contributing to discussions, and engaging in the inquiry process with other learners. Learners participating with other learners to gain understanding and build knowledge is an essential step in developing the mindset of Collaborate in learners.

Collaborate in Action: Digital Citizenship

In January 2013, Pulitzer Prize–winning journalist and National Geographic Fellow Paul Salopek set out on a 21,000-mile walking journey across the world to trace the first steps of human migration out of Africa, across continents to the tip of South America. Salopek is engaging in the process of slow journalism to make connections with people and tell their stories as he documents the changes in the world caused by climate change, technology, human migration, and the human experience. He is documenting his travels through National Geographic's Out of Eden Walk website, social media including Instagram and Twitter, and articles in *National Geographic* magazine.

Salopek also is connecting with learners and connecting learners with each other through the Out of Eden Learn program coordinated by the Harvard Graduate School of Education's Project Zero. The Out of Eden Learn program is a "custom built, social media platform" where "students of similar ages from diverse geographical and socioeconomic settings come together for collective learning experiences" (Out of Eden Learn, n.d.). Learners from around the world are placed in digital cohorts to engage in online and off-line activities that ask them to slow down, look at the world around them, share their ideas and perspectives with each other, and engage in thoughtful discussion through the digital platform. As the Out of Eden Learn organizers state, "In this era of interconnection, disconnection, and rapid change, it is vitally important to offer young people opportunities to dialogue and build understandings with peers from different backgrounds" (Out of Eden Learn, n.d.). The goals of this project are for learners to slow down and interact with their community and world, to make deep connections, and to develop a more complete view of our world through digital conversations with others.

Connecting with Other Learners in a Digital World

Among the deepest connections that learners make in this project are the connections with other learners through the digital platform in their online "walking parties." The Out of Eden Learn secure social platform is where learners share their work with other members in the cohort, read the works of the other learners, and then engage in online conversations and collaborations based on the work they are sharing. The Out of Eden Learn platform provides a dialogue toolkit (https:// learn.outofedenwalk.com/dialogue-toolkit). This toolkit offers tools for learners to engage deeply with others through the online platform—more deeply than typical online interactions involving a Like button. The platform facilitates learners':

- Making connections with others' work
- Offering feedback on what they appreciate about the work
- Making a connection with their own lives and work
- Probing deeply with queries that will help questioners better understand another perspective
- Extending their own thoughts to offer other learners a new perspective or take a conversation to another step with a deeper connection

All these tools help young people engage in meaningful learning experiences in a digital world. The learners most likely will never meet in person, but the Out of Eden Learn platform is a way for them to make connections with people outside their community and country while gaining new perspectives, feeling like part of the global community, and growing by sharing their work with an authentic audience. This program allows learners to "actively [contribute] to group discussions" in a digital world (AASL 2018, Learner III.D.1). Learners are listening to, responding to, and learning from not only their classmates but also their "walking partners" from around the world.

Learners Mapping Their World

One of the first footsteps (projects) in which learners participate on the Out of Eden Learn platform is the neighborhood walk. Learners read one of Paul Salopek's milestones and learn more about his journey. He shares what it means to slow down and really engage in slow looking, to make deep connections with what is observed and with what story the neighborhood tells about a people, culture, or community.

Learners are then assigned the task of taking a slow walk around their own neighborhood, mapping out what they see and what stands out to them as telling a story about themselves and the community they call home. Learners spend a week drawing their maps and documenting landmarks that are important to residents of their neighborhood, their families, and themselves.

Next, learners write a couple of paragraphs telling the story of their neighborhood through their art and their words and then post their work to the Out of Eden Learn platform.

Then learners read and look at the work of their walking partners from around the world. Learners recognize similarities with other learners who live in different types of communities. Even though learners in our school live in an urban area in the United States, they notice that so much of what is important to them is equally important to their walking partners who live in rural areas. Our learners read and think about different climates and cultures and, aided by the prompts in the dialogue toolkit, are able to make deep connections, receive feedback on their work, and edit and rework their writings and illustrations based on the discussions with other learners to become better storytellers and writers.

Receiving feedback and collaboration from peers not in our school is invaluable. The experiences are authentic, and learners are engaged in their work because the feedback and reflections come from learners their own age and from peers whom they have not known their whole school lives. The program helps learners to "[recognize] learning as a social responsibility" (AASL 2018, Learner III.D.2.). They are able to deepen their understanding and knowledge of the world through their communications with other learners. The Out of Eden Learn project is an excellent example of a digital learning environment that engages learners in collaborative experiences that build and grow their collaboration skills.

Zooming Out on the Domains

After looking at each Domain individually to better understand how its unique characteristics lend to developing the Collaborate mindset, it is also important to recognize that developing collaborative qualities in learners is fluid. Learners will engage in the collaborative process, engaging with all the Domains in one project. This big-picture view is important to examine as school librarians are dissecting the AASL Standards. Looking at developing collaboration qualities in learners from different angles, zooming in and out, to see different views should help school librarians as they seek opportunities to cultivate the mindset of Collaborate in learners.

COLLABORATE IN ACTION: FIRST-GRADE DOT DAY

The first-grade educators and I were looking for more opportunities to collaborate on the first-grade curriculum goals for literacy, storytelling, and the central topic of "community." I was looking for more opportunities to connect the work of literacy skills with a collaborative building and making project that would be a deep dive into a story and allow learners to build new knowledge. International Dot Day had been a part of the curriculum for several years. The day is a global celebration of creativity, courage, and collaboration inspired by the book *The Dot* by Peter H. Reynolds and started by educator Terry Shay on September 15, 2009 ("Get Started!" 2019). Over the past decade the event has grown into a day of celebration at public and school libraries, community centers, and classrooms around the world. The focus of the day is on engaging learners in creative pursuits that encourage them to make their mark on the world with art, creativity, and collaboration. Over the years the first-grade team and I had shared the book with learners, discussed the ideas in the story, and encouraged learners to create art projects inspired by the characters. This time, we wanted to design a project that would connect more deeply to the idea of being a classroom community and that would develop the skills of collaboration in learners while still making connections to literacy and storytelling. Our work together was a way for us to "[create] a learning environment in which learners understand that learning is a social responsibility" (AASL 2018, School Librarian III.D.2.), with each stage of the project focusing on collaboration.

The project started with reading *The Dot* aloud, sharing the story of Vashti, a young learner who does not think that she is good at art. She sits at her desk with a blank sheet of paper in front of her and then informs the educator that she just can't draw; she's not good at it. The educator tells her to just make a mark, so Vashti takes her pen and makes one small dot in the middle of the page. The educator looks at the paper and then tells Vashti to sign it. The next time Vashti is in art class she sees her dot hanging on the wall in a beautiful gold frame and she thinks to herself "I can do better than that!" Vashti starts making all kinds of dots, big, small, in different colors, and using different materials. At the end of the story, Vashti hosts an art exhibit with all her work. A young boy comments to Vashti that she is such a great artist. He says, "I can't draw a straight line with a ruler." And Vashti says, "Show me." The boy makes a squiggly line on a black sheet of paper, and Vashti tells him, "Now sign it!" The story is simple but deep, told in just one to two sentences per page.

Learners discussed the structure of the story, including the beginning, middle, and end of the story, the setting, and the characters. This discussion was a connection to literacy skills and shared language that was familiar to learners in the first-grade classroom when books were shared. Next, learners focused on the character of Vashti, working in small groups to share the words they would use to describe her at the beginning of the story and the words to describe her at the end of the story. Members of each group then shared their thoughts and ideas with the whole class. Learners realized that more than one group thought of the same traits and ideas; they also learned new ideas and connections from each other. First graders were "developing new understandings through engagement in a learning group" (AASL 2018, Learner III.A.2.). In the final step of the data-collection and information-gathering stage, learners thought about how, like Vashti, they made their marks with art and how they also make their marks on other people's hearts. Learners talked about how they impact other members of their community when they act with kindness and positivity in their classroom and school community. The whole class shared information as learners were "actively contributing to group discussions" (AASL 2018, Learner III.D.1.).

Make Your Mark on People's Hearts

First graders collaboratively developed this list connecting the story of *The Dot* to their lives and identifying ways they made their marks with art and on other people's hearts.

- Helping classmates stay on task
- Telling someone she did a good job
- Being kind to each other
- Inviting someone to play
- Showing someone a new skill or how to make something
- Helping on a project
- Thinking of a kind gift for someone else
- Following the rules
- Asking someone if he is okay and helping if he is hurt
- Sharing with others
- Helping to fix something if you accidentally break it
- Paying attention and listening to educators
- Doing your best work
- Respecting others' space
- Not being silly at the wrong time
- Helping educators not make mistakes
- Making something and giving it to someone
- Helping with jobs in the classroom
- Talking through problems
- Helping people clean up
- Taking someone who is hurt to the nurse
- Helping get stuff down from the high shelf for someone
- Giving someone a second chance
- Standing up for others
- Cleaning up the classroom
- Offering helping hands
- Sharing books

Think and Grow: Learners Define the Qualities of a Collaborator

The next step in the project was for learners to think about a time they had worked or created with someone else, worked on a team, or worked with other learners and had a positive experience. These first graders shared why it was a good experience not only for themselves but for the other members of their group. Using sticky notes, they collected words to describe the experience. Then learners read their classmates' notes and started to create groups of similar words and themes. This silent sorting process helped learners recognize larger themes and qualities that are important for collaboration to be successful. The sorting process was a way of "challenging learners to work with others to broaden and deepen understandings" (AASL 2018, School Librarian III.A.1.). Engaging in a silent sorting was also a way for first graders "to actively contribute to group discussions" (AASL 2018, School Librarian III.D.1.), a way that allowed introverted learners to think about and process their ideas and contribute to the final list and allowed extraverted learners to slow down and think through a process without sharing out loud.

Once all the words were sorted into groups, learners engaged in a group discussion to identify themes and titles for the groups. The final list included five themes:

- Listen
- Share ideas
- Everyone agrees
- Everyone has a part
- Everyone is kind

These five themes became the collaborator qualities on which learners would focus in the next step. This process made many connections to the learning goals of the first-grade and school library curricula, including the following:

- Making deep connections to literature and the learners' lives
- Developing a better understanding of story structure and the elements of a book
- Recognizing what it means to be a member of a community
- Being conscious of effective ways learners work and engage with peers and others in the school

Think: Collaborative Problem Solving

Once learners had established the five themes that they felt were essential to a positive collaborative experience, the next step was to put those ideas to the test by engaging in a challenge. Learners formed small groups and were challenged to work together to design and build a working art robot. Learners could use any of the materials in the school library's makerspace, including cardboard, plastic containers, paper towel rolls, and the like, connected with Little Bits circuits and markers to make the robot move and draw. In the final step, each group's robot would contribute to a collaborative piece of art to be displayed in the first-grade hallway and shared with the whole community. Empowering first graders with the decision-making process was a way of "organizing learner groups for decision making and problem solving" (AASL 2018, School Librarian III.A.3.).

In their small groups, the learners' first step was to set their group norms. Focusing on the five collaborator qualities, each group set rules and norms to establish how the group would ensure that every member listened, shared ideas, agreed, had a part, and was kind. Learners were instructed that when a conflict in their group happened as they were designing and building, they had to consult their group norms to figure out a way to resolve their conflict and collaborate. The agreed-upon norms were written down, and each group member signed the sheet to show that they all agreed.

First-Grade Collaborator Qualities

Here is an example of the group norms decided by the first graders and signed by all group members:

- Listen
    - Look at the person who is talking.
    - Show the person that you are focusing by not messing around.
    - Respond to what the person says.

- Share ideas
    - Tell the others your idea.
    - Plan together.
    - Listen and talk—"huddling up and making a plan."

- Everyone agrees
    - Compromise—sometimes we might have to give something up.
    - Use rock/paper/scissors.
    - Use eenie-meenie-miney-mo in rounds.

- Everyone has a part
    - If you know how to do something, teach others in the group.
    - Take turns.
    - Listen and communicate.

- Everyone is kind
    - Listen
    - Always have a smile.
    - Let others go first.

Signed by John, Lilia, and Griffin

Think, Create, Share, and Grow: Building Together

Next came the planning and design stage. Learners explored the materials they had to work with and mapped out how they would build their art robots. Learners used their collaborative group norms to work together and plan. The group norms established a way for learners to "solve problems by soliciting and responding to feedback from others" (AASL 2018, Learner III.C.1.) as they negotiated and compromised with each other to design one robot. Then they worked together to build and test their robots. All the groups had to redesign their robots—some added too many markers, some had to change the placement of their motors, and some had to change the position of the markers to make the robot move. All the learners had to test their first design, look at the results, and then think about what they needed to change to make their robot work. They learned from their first iterations and made adjustments. None of the robots worked on the first try, so the first graders needed to learn from what they had done and try again. When the art robots didn't work, learners worked through the challenges together, "deciding to solve problems informed by group interaction" (AASL 2018, Learner III.A.3.). Throughout this project, learners had to listen to each other, come to agreements, and engage in social learning. First graders were "establishing connections with other learners to build on their own prior knowledge and create new knowledge" (AASL 2018, Learner III.B.2.).

For the final step, each group in the class placed its working robot on a large sheet of white paper, and each robot contributed to the collaborative artwork. Everyone in the class signed the artwork to take ownership and show pride in what they had accomplished collaboratively. The first graders were so proud of the final work their group did and of the work of the whole grade level. They recognized that no one would have been able to accomplish this project alone and that, by working with others, they were "recognizing learning as a social responsibility" (AASL 2018, Learner III.D.2.). The first graders' artwork was displayed in the hallway to share their work with the whole school community. The collaboration qualities that learners developed were displayed in the school library and classrooms and were used in collaborative projects throughout the school year to remind learners how to work together.

COLLABORATIVE EDUCATOR CONNECTIONS

The goals of this project were to develop collaborative qualities in learners and to encourage the learners to be engaged and invested in those qualities. The Dot Day project accomplished those goals. This project met many of the AASL Standards' Learner Competencies along with the School Librarian Competencies and the School Library Alignments. Throughout this project, I was engaging in work with the first-grade team and with the structure and schedule of the project to cultivate a more collaborative environment. During our planning, the first-grade team and I made connections between what was happening in the classroom and what was required by the curriculum. We partnered "to scaffold learning and organize learner groups to broaden and deepen understanding" (AASL 2018, School Library III.A.1.). We were engaging in a collaborative process in which the first-grade educators felt that their voices were being heard and that their curriculum was being enhanced with the Dot Day project. Both the first-grade team and I were "modeling respect for diverse perspectives to guide the inquiry process" (AASL 2018, School Librarian

III.C.2.) in the creation and execution of this project. In addition to the first graders having practiced the qualities of effective collaborators and developed understanding of the social nature of learning, the first-grade educators and I were "creating a learning environment in which learners understand that learning is a social responsibility" (AASL 2018, School Librarian III.D.2.). This project was successful because everyone—educators and first graders—collaborated and worked together to make it a success.

Questions for the Reflective Practitioner

1 As I design and plan lessons, how are the Domains an essential framework for the bigger picture of mindsets essential to Collaborate?

2 How might I and co-educators design lessons and projects in which the Domains of Think, Create, Share, and Grow are woven into the fabric of the learning to help learners develop the mindset of Collaborate?

3 How might I give learners ownership in the inquiry process to further develop a collaborative mindset?

4 How might I reach out to fellow educators, across departments or districts, to design lessons that engage learners in collaborative work?

5

Promoting Learner Voice and Choice

reating a culture in which learners are engaged and feel their voices are heard is an important step in developing a mindset of collaboration in learners. To collaborate, school librarians must develop trusting relationships with other educators; learners need to develop trusting relationships with school librarians as well. For learners to trust educators and be willing to be open and share their learning, their struggles, and their successes, learners need to know that they have a collaborative role in their own learning. Learners' relationships with school librarians and other educators are a part of developing a collaborative relationship. Learners need to be engaged in work knowing that their voices are being heard, that they have a part in designing what they are learning.

Collaboration is a social learning process. "When learners work together in group- and team-based situations, they are able to solve problems together that they would not be able to solve independently" (AASL 2018, 86). The foundation of Collaborate calls on school librarians to design a school library learning environment that encourages learners to collaborate and to develop the mindset of a collaborator. An essential step in creating a culture of collaboration in a school is for school librarians to collaborate with learners in the development of the learning environment. School librarians need to create the framework for learning, define learning goals, scaffold, and have measurable outcomes of learner growth. However, school librarians need to do these within the context of being facilitators and lifelong learners themselves, not as the keepers of all knowledge. To be effective, the educator-learner relationship must be a collaborative one.

School Librarians Learning Alongside Learners

The AASL Standards call for learners to "participate in personal, social, and intellectual networks by establishing connections with other learners" (AASL 2018, Learner III.B.2.). These connections with other learners should include the school librarian as a co-learner and a member of the learners' learning network. Part of collaborating with learners and giving them voice and choice is being open to the ways that learners choose to make their learning visible—even if those methods are unfamiliar to the school librarian. The collaboration and co-learning among student learners and educators begin with conversation. When school libraries are learner-centered, learners are engaged in the process and feel empowered in their own learning. As Gever Tulley, founder of Brightworks School in San Francisco, said, "The world doesn't need more graduates with good grades: What the world needs is voracious, self-directed learners with the creative capacity to see the problems of the world as puzzles, and the tenacity to work on them, even in the face of adversity" (Clapp 2017, 9).

The AASL Standards express the need for learners to "actively [contribute] to group discussions" and "[recognize] learning as a social responsibility" (AASL 2018, Learner III.D.1, III.D.2.). To help learners develop these Competencies, school librarians and other educators must provide learning opportunities that accomplish the following goals:

- Engage learners in the "what and why" of the planning process
- Give learners a voice in the design of units, lessons, and projects, and in how learning products will be created and shared
- Stimulate learners' curiosity
- Allow learners to participate in conversation and discussion about what they are learning and why

School librarians can collaborate with learners in the designing of the learning process and still have boundaries and a learning framework. Collaboration with learners in the process is possible, and school librarians can still have measurable outcomes and documentation of learning. Learner voice and choice can be a driving force in the learning and still meet state and national standards. When school librarians engage in the collaborative process with learners, they are making connections between the AASL Standards for learners and those for school librarians.

COLLABORATE IN ACTION: LITERATURE AND ART PROJECT

Kate Tabor, a seventh-grade English educator, has her learners focus on voice and storytelling in her curriculum. She wanted her learners to engage in an in-depth project combining art in the community, storytelling, and technology. A wide selection of art is displayed around the school campus. The seventh graders spend time identifying the artwork around the building and thinking about three questions:

- How might we tell the story of the art on campus?
- How might we encourage people to interact with the art in nonphysical ways?
- How might we share the art with the community?

This English educator was looking for an engaging way for seventh-grade learners to share their knowledge and learning in a visible and collaborative way. Tabor paired with Annette Lesak, the middle school librarian, to plan the project and to use the materials in the school library's makerspace. When these two educators talked through the unit, the goals, and outcomes, they knew learner voice and choice were going to be key to the success of the project and truly allow for collaboration in learner groups. The English educator and the school librarian established a framework and process that they hoped would amplify learners' voices and lead to a collaborative process for learners.

Think and Create: Creating Interest-Based Collaborative Groups

The English educator introduced the project by showing her classes examples of creative ways that art museums use technology to engage visitors and prospective visitors with the art collections. She then highlighted some options for her seventh graders to think about, including a BuzzFeed-style quiz, Scratch coding, and Claymation. The school librarian shared many of the tools in the library's makerspace, including stop-motion animation, 360-degree cameras, augmented-reality apps, and more. Learners could also write short stories or comic books incorporating pieces of art in the narratives. By offering learners different options, the team of educators was "modeling the use of a variety of communication tools and resources" (AASL 2018, School Librarian III.B.1.).

The next step was to turn the project over to the seventh graders. These learners were given time to brainstorm an idea and design a pitch for how they would highlight the artwork around the building using some of the tools mentioned or an idea they identified on their own.

Next, learners who had a pitch idea documented their plan on large pieces of paper (which did not include the learners' names) that were posted around the room. Learners had a chance to explore all the options and add their names to the idea they were most interested in working on. The process was silent, so it was not about discussing with friends which project they were working on but focused on learners engaging in a process in which they were interested. This process determined the groups, and the originator of the idea was the group leader. The English educator said this process created groups of learners that did not usually collaborate and provided an opportunity for learners who were not usually leaders to step forward. By following this process to create collaborative teams, she was "organizing learner groups for decision making and problem solving" (AASL 2018, School Librarian III.A.3.). She also commented that this process allowed learners to find their voice and group leaders to be seen in a new role and share skills they might not usually have the opportunity to highlight in the classroom. The process focused on "challenging learners to work with others to broaden and deepen understandings" (AASL 2018, School Librarian III.A.1.).

Create and Grow: Exploring Ideas Together

The two educators gave learners a framework for the process and a timeline for work, but the rest of the process was up to the collaborative groups as they organized their work and determined what they would do to be successful. As learners pursued the project, the educators were co-learners and facilitators as the seventh graders worked through technology challenges or needed advice on next steps. Learners were not focused on making sure everything was perfect for an end grade.

Tabor reflected that "my students would say to me, 'Let me show you this,' not 'Is this okay or correct?'" They were talking through challenges with an adult co-learner, not looking for validation that the project was following an educator's checklist. The fact that the school librarian and the classroom educator did not have a set idea of how the projects would turn out gave learners the freedom to drive the project. The English educator also said, "I wasn't focused on the end product because I didn't have a set idea of what the project would be. This changed the nature of the learner engagement with the educators; it was collaborative, not transactional. It was about the process, not the end product or grade." Because the seventh graders were given the time and autonomy to work through the collaboration and decision process, they could explore various options for sharing their knowledge, working with technology, consulting with the collaborating educators to talk through ideas, and then designing and working with their group. In this process, the seventh graders and the educators were learning from each other. They were "establishing connections with other learners to build on their own prior knowledge and create new knowledge" (AASL 2018, Learner III.B.2.). Challenges and disagreements happened, and learners were given the time and space to work through those as well. Taking a step back, the educators let learners struggle and allowed learners to navigate and rethink the challenges as well as negotiate among themselves to solve any conflict. Learners and educators were "recognizing learning as a social responsibility" (AASL 2018, Learner III.D.2.).

Think and Grow: Learners as Educators

Very rarely does everything work the way it is planned. Some groups had a plan mapped out, but when they were creating their projects, they ran into issues and challenges and had to think and rethink to create the project that they wanted. This circumstance presented opportunities for seventh graders to step into the role of coach.

For example, several groups decided to create BuzzFeed-inspired quizzes about the art on campus. A learner in one of these groups was a BuzzFeed expert and understood how to create the algorithm to generate the results. Another group was really struggling with the same process, and the learner who excelled was able to coach the other team and help those learners be successful. The English educator said, "It was wonderful to see this student take a leadership role but more to see her coach the other group and help them work through the challenges, not just tell them how to fix it but to teach them how to do it themselves." This project offered opportunities for learners to "[decide] to solve problems informed by group interaction" (AASL 2018, Learner III.A.3.) and "actively [contribute] to group discussions" (AASL 2018, Learner III.D.1.).

Share: Sharing Learners' Work

Learners not only shared their work with their classmates, they also created a website to share their work with the larger school community and produced Instagram and Twitter feeds to share their work with a larger authentic audience, adding another element to the social and collaborative nature of the project. The English educator reflected that sharing their work with a larger audience and receiving feedback from beyond the walls of the classroom "engaged students even more in the project" and led them to "see their work [as] very meaningful." This sharing within the school and beyond its walls is another way that learners can "[solicit] and [respond] to feedback from others" (AASL 2018, Learner III.C.1.).

If learners are to develop the qualities of collaborators, school librarians and other educators must give them the opportunity to develop these skills. Adults cannot be the ones scripting the projects, being the experts on the technology, problem solving for learners, and not giving them the opportunity to fail and rethink and rework. Learners are never going to become collaborators unless they are given the opportunity to collaborate.

COLLABORATE IN ACTION: PASSION PROJECTS

Annette Lesak, a middle school librarian, was looking for a way to bring more middle schoolers into the school library and use the maker resources that were added to its space. She had read about 20 percent time, genius hour, and passion projects. The concept of 20 percent time is based on a program that was started at Google during the early days of the company. Google founders Larry Page and Sergey Brin referenced 20 percent time in their IPO letter in 2004: "We encourage our employees, in addition to their regular projects, to spend 20% of their time working on what they think will most benefit Google. This empowers them to be more creative and innovative. Many of our significant advances have happened in this manner" (D'Onfro 2015). Google is just one of many companies and industries that embraced the idea of giving employees the time and space to pursue something they were passionate about.

The idea spread from the corporate and academic worlds to schools. *The Passion-Driven Classroom: A Framework for Teaching and Learning* by Angela Maiers and

Amy Sandvold was the first publication to share the idea of genius hour or passion projects in the education setting (Kesler 2019). Many schools offer genius hour and passion projects as opportunities for learners to work on something they are passionate about.

This school librarian decided to offer her middle school learners the opportunity to do passion projects, not only so they could pursue a passion but also so they could have a guided learning opportunity with set goals, use of the design process, research and planning, and a chance to collaborate.

Think and Grow: Brainstorming and Do Sheets

To increase learners' chances of completing their projects, this middle school librarian mapped out the eight-week commitment with a mix of independent group time for work on the projects and a structure that helped learners manage their time and work. At Advisory (similar to homeroom), she shared the opportunity to do passion projects, and interested learners signed up to attend the lunchtime organization meetings to start the project. In many cases, learners did not start with a particular idea in mind. To spark creativity, the school librarian shared some projects, materials, and technology that could be used. The middle schoolers thought about what they were interested in, brainstormed together, and bounced ideas off each other.

Once individuals or groups had decided what they wanted to focus on, they completed a Do Sheet provided by the school librarian. This sheet included a timeline of goals and a checklist of what had to be accomplished to meet each goal. The Do Sheet was divided into sections. First, what was the Quest or the goal to be met or the end product to be created? Next, what were the Dos, or the steps that learners would need to take to complete the Quest? Finally, what defined Done for each Do step? When would a task be completed, allowing the learner to move forward to the next step? The Do Sheets documented learners' "desire to broaden and deepen understandings" (AASL 2018, Learner III.A.1.) by having learners share their process for collecting knowledge to complete their project.

The school librarian also created a Team Drive in Google for learners to share their Do Sheets and document their progress. By sharing their work, learners were "developing new understandings through engagement in a learning group" (AASL 2018, Learner III.A.2.). The Team Drive was a way that other learners in the passion project group could share ideas to help their fellow classmates on different projects. Learners also shared their plans and ideas for the passion projects on the whiteboard wall in the school library, publicly sharing their ideas with each other and creating a collaborative community related to the projects so that learners could support each other and "[recognize] learning as a social responsibility" (AASL 2018, Learner III.D.2.).

Share: Time, Space, and Connections

Throughout the eight-week period, learners were allowed to work in the school library during lunch periods and after school to complete their projects. Learners kept track of their progress on their Do Sheets and talked to the school librarian when they had challenges, needed more information or research on their process, or needed help with obtaining materials. The school librarian also established weekly check-in meetings with the whole group, an essential step in creating a collaborative community of support that helped learners stay on track, overcome challenges, and help each other work through problems, offering advice and feedback. Learners also came together to encourage each other; when a learner or group completed a Do on their Do Sheet, Lesak rang a gong to celebrate the milestone. These meetings established a collaborative community for the group and offered opportunities for learners to "[solicit] and [respond] to feedback from others" (AASL 2018, Learner III.C.1.).

The eight-week timeframe was also an important part of the project; learners had set start and stop dates for the projects, a strategy that helped keep them focused, organized, and on task. Some learners did not complete their projects in the allotted time but still felt part of a collaborative group and took it upon themselves to continue to work independently after the passion project cycle ended. The school librarian reflected that learners were able to pursue a passion and interest in a "low stakes" process. She said, "They were excited to learn a process, and, in some cases, fail and rethink their learning but without the pressure of a grade attached." This project was a pure learning experience that was about the enjoyment of being a life-long learner. Middle schoolers learned about themselves as collaborators, how to manage and organize tasks with other learners, and how to share their work with a group. All who participated became invested in celebrating and supporting the other learners.

Passion Project in Action: Dorodango

The passion projects required the school librarian to be open to learning new techniques with her learners, in addition to using her more-traditional librarian skills in teaching research and information-seeking skills. Learners were interested in a wide array of projects, some of which, such as podcasting and sewing, required skills familiar to this educator. However, some of the projects involved materials and skills she knew nothing about—and the learners' knowledge wasn't much more. For example, one seventh grader, Jake, was interested in dorodango, a Japanese art form in which earth and water are molded to create a delicate, shiny sphere. Lesak and Jake set out to collaborate and learn more together. They started by doing research and collecting resources. They both "[demonstrated] their desire to broaden and deepen understandings" (AASL 2018, Learner III.A.1.) when they met to talk about what they had learned and map out what resources Jake would need to make the dorodango. These collaborative meetings helped both of them develop "new under-standings through engagement in a learning group" (AASL 2018, Learner III.A.2.).

When Jake ran into some problems and his dorodango started to crack, the two learners searched websites and YouTube to see how they might fix the cracks or use different materials to make a dorodango. They worked together, "deciding to solve problems informed by group interaction" (AASL 2018, Learner III.A.3.) as they collaborated, shared ideas, and talked through challenges together to accomplish a goal.

Throughout the process the learner and the educator kept in contact in a vari-ety of ways: in-person conversations, e-mails, shared documents on Google Drive, and videos on FlipGrid. They were "using a variety of communication tools and resources" (AASL 2018, Learner III.B.1.) to accomplish their goals, stay on task, and stay in touch.

Jake and Lesak worked through the challenges of making this art by sharing and talking and "soliciting and responding to feedback from others" (AASL 2018, Learner III.C.1.). They talked about what was working and what was not working. Even though Lesak was the educator, she was not in the position of expert. She received feedback from Jake, and he received feedback from her; they were collab-orators and co-learners.

Both Jake and Lesak grew in this process. They learned more about themselves and each other as they worked to learn more about making a dorodango, search-ing for resources and dealing with frustrations. This whole process would not have been successful if they had not worked together by "actively contributing to group discussions" (AASL 2018, Learner III.D.1.). Jake was able to pursue this opportunity because his school librarian was open to allowing learners to pursue their interests and passions.

Passion Project in Action: Soap Making and Social Entrepreneurship

During another passion project cycle, a group of sixth graders were interested in learning to make soap. Their goals were to learn the process, design different types of soap, and then establish a platform to sell their products, with all the profits going to a local children's hospital.

The learners were very passionate about supporting the work of the hospital as a way to share their work and help others. Therefore, part of the process was to deter-mine prices that would cover the cost of materials and the donation to the hospital.

Lesak helped the learners work through the process, which they mapped out and shared on a Do Sheet, from finding research resources to learning how to make soap, add different ingredients to enhance the fragrance or change the type of soap, and mold the soaps into various shapes. The learners also considered how to pack-age their soaps to make them attractive to prospective buyers.

As the learners worked through their process, they designed and redesigned their soap making, learning more about what did and did not work. They also learned more about themselves and about how this group of friends worked and did not work as collaborators. Team members divided up tasks and worked to overcome some of the challenges they encountered as collaborators, keeping each other accountable and learning in what role each member was the most effective and successful. The school librarian worked with the learners to help them negotiate and compromise. Through this process, the sixth graders were learning "respect for diverse perspectives to guide the inquiry process" (AASL 2018, School Librarian III.C.2.).

The school librarian also had the learners research the Lurie Children's Hospital to understand the work the hospital did and how the funds raised would support that work. The sixth graders learned that they had a responsibility to understand and to educate others about the organization to which they were donating the funds. Meeting this responsibility was part of the learners' "demonstrating their desire to broaden and deepen understandings" (AASL 2018, Learner III.A.1.). Before they started selling the soaps, the sixth graders organized a teach-in about Lurie Children's Hospital, explaining the mission of the organization and what the funds would support. The event took place during lunch, and middle school learners, educators, and the head of the middle school were invited to hear more about the hospital and its mission. With this teach-in, Lesak was "creating a learning environment in which learners understand that learning is a social responsibility" (AASL 2018, School Librarian III.D.2.).

The group worked to get their soaps ready for the sale, produced signs to post around the school, got help from their families to have money to make change, set up tables, and prepared to sell the soaps. Group members were excited to sell their soaps and received authentic feedback from their customers about what soaps were the most successful. At the sales event, learners also answered questions and shared information about Lurie Children's Hospital. This public event was very meaningful for the learners as they demonstrated how to "[solicit] and [respond] to feedback from others" (AASL 2018, Learner III.C.1.), sold soaps, and took orders for more while fielding questions.

Learners were responsible for the follow-up after the sale, ensuring that the soaps people had ordered were completed and delivered. They were very proud of the work they did and excited when the school librarian exchanged the cash for a school check made out to the hospital. The learners wrote letters to the hospital about the work they did and the sale they organized to raise the funds. This passion project was truly a collaborative learning experience for everyone in the school, and everyone involved "[recognized] learning as a social responsibility" (AASL 2018, Learner III.D.2.).

Questions for the Reflective Practitioner

1 In what ways do I already offer voice and choice to learners to develop collaboration skills?

2 What are more ways that I can collaborate with learners to model collaboration and also be their co-learner?

3 What can I do to advocate with other educators for giving voice and choice to learners and to support a more social and collaborative learning environment?

6

Collaborating at Different Grade Levels

arol Dweck's groundbreaking book *Mindset: The New Psychology of Success* first presented the ideas of fixed mindset and growth mindset. A fixed mindset "is the belief that one's abilities are carved in stone," and a growth mindset is "the belief that one's skills and abilities can be cultivated through effort and perseverance" (Gross-Loh 2016). The release of Dweck's book brought the idea of these mindsets to parents, to people in business and industry, and— especially—to the education world. Educators have embraced the idea of cultivating growth mindsets in 21st-century learners as an essential asset for expanding their knowledge, fostering new skills, facing new challenges, persisting after failure, and being prepared for life in an ever-changing world.

Over the last several years, Dweck has re-released her book with updates to educate the population about what a growth mindset really is, in contrast to what she calls a "false growth mindset." She says that some people oversimplify the idea and focus only on effort. Educators' simple praising of effort is not effective (Gross-Loh 2016). To move beyond a "false growth mindset," educators must know that the growth mindset is also about strategies. Dweck says, "Effective teachers who actually have classrooms full of children with a growth mindset are always supporting children's learning strategies and showing how strategies created that success" (Gross-Loh 2016).

Developing collaboration skills in learners requires an approach similar to that for developing a growth mindset. To develop a collaborative mindset, learners must be shown effective strategies and have the time to expand and grow their collaboration skills throughout their school years. Learners need to be given opportunities to fail at collaboration, reflect on failures, and redesign new paths to success. School librarians and other educators need to create development markers and assessment tools to define what successful collaboration looks like developmentally at different age levels and to document growth over time to ensure that learners are developing competencies in collaboration.

AASL Standards Learning Continuum

The AASL Standards provide a framework for collaboration for school librarians to incorporate in their curriculum goals and outcomes for learners. AASL states that the Key Commitment of Collaborate is for learners to "work effectively with others to broaden perspectives and work toward common goals" (AASL 2018, 85). This commitment is framed in the context of the four Domains: Think, Create, Share, and Grow. Within each of these Domains, specific Competencies are identified for learners and school librarians, and Alignments are given for school libraries. When school librarians look at the Domains and think about ways to foster growth and development of the Collaborate mindset in learners, these Domains should not be viewed as specific linear steps from Think to Create to Share to Grow. Instead, teach-

FIGURE 6.1 /
The continuous cycle of AASL Standards Domains

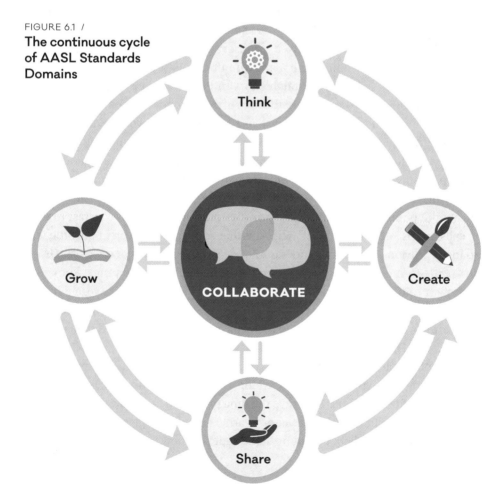

ing and learning in the Domains should be viewed as a continuous cycle (figure 6.1), with learners flowing back and forth between the Domains through various entry points and connections over the years.

In an inquiry process, learners might start in Think and "[develop] new understandings though engagement in a learning group" (AASL 2018, Learner III.A.2.), such as a small-group collaboration on a topic. Then learners could move to the Domain of Create, "using a variety of communication tools and resources" (AASL 2018, Learner III.B.1.) to expand their understanding of a topic. This step, in turn, could lead to the development of more questions and insights, returning learners to the Think Domain as they are again "developing new understandings through engagement in a learning group" (AASL 2018, Learner III.A.2.). At this point in the process, learners could then move to the Share Domain, "soliciting and responding to feedback from others" (AASL 2018, Learner III.C.1.), and the feedback that learners receive could lead them back to the Think Domain and to "deciding to solve problems informed by group interaction" (AASL 2018, Learner III.A.3.). In addition, as they explore feedback and questions, learners might connect to the Grow Domain Competency of "recognizing learning as a social responsibility" (AASL 2018, Learner III.D.2.; figure 6.2).

FIGURE 6.2 /

Example of the flow between Domains

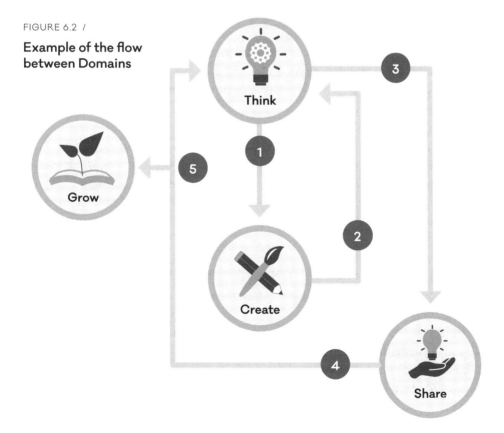

In addition to viewing learners' progress as they develop a collaborative mindset and Collaborate Competencies as a fluid, nonlinear process, school librarians and other educators should view teaching and learning within all the Shared Foundations as a process with many possible entry points. Learners will enter their development of Competencies in the AASL Standards at different Domains and advance through the Competencies at a varied pace throughout their school careers.

School librarians also need to develop assessments and documentation that demonstrate the growth of learners as collaborators as they develop this mindset and the Competencies that come with it. Evidence of developing a Collaborate mindset and the Competencies that accompany it becomes more sophisticated and complex as learners grow and can look different among the learners in any class. School librarians and other educators need a learning trajectory for Collaborate, so as learners move through school, they can identify various levels of collaboration, using the lens of the AASL Standards and Domains as a way to identify goals and expectations for learners.

Collaborate Learning Trajectory

What follows is a learning trajectory divided by grade levels: preschool to second grade, third to fifth grade, sixth to eighth grade, and ninth to twelfth grade. Each of the grade-level discussions is followed by a learning trajectory chart that is structured using the AASL Standards and Domains with bullet points documenting learner goals for that grade level. A sample unit or project is also documented illustrating the goals in action. Developing learning trajectories is an exercise that school librarians and districts need to explore specific to the needs of their learning communities and curricula. The Collaborate learning trajectory charts provided here are meant to be used merely as reference guides for school librarians to consult or to modify to suit their learning community. As school librarians evaluate their curriculum through the lens of the AASL Standards and create custom learning trajectory charts for their learners, these charts may be useful examples for implementing the Shared Foundation of Collaborate and cultivating learners' mindsets across school libraries and districts.

COLLABORATIVE MINDSET: PRESCHOOL–SECOND GRADE

When working with the youngest learners, collaboration can often be a challenge. Many learners need direction and help as they navigate group work and whole-class conversations. They are just learning to be aware of others, developing listening skills, and facing the challenges of sharing time and space with their classmates. Early elementary learners are also just learning to read and write. This circumstance creates added challenges when school librarians and other educators are attempting to foster learners' development of the mindset of Collaborate and assess growth in learners as they move back and forth in the Domains (table 6.1).

Collaborate in Action: Exploring the Dinosaur World

Kindergarten is the time that learners start to delve into different topics of inter-est, begin to be able to distinguish between fact and fiction, and make connections with their background knowledge about a subject area. Several times a year, I work with the kindergarten educators to find a topic that the learners are interested in exploring. In the classroom and the school library, learners brainstorm a list of top-ics in which they are interested. The classroom educators and I also look at what books our kindergarten learners are frequently checking out of the school library to help us focus on a topic. One class expressed interest in dinosaurs; learners shared this as a topic of interest and constantly checked out dinosaur books, and even the learners who did not focus on dinosaurs as a topic did check out books about ani-mals and nature. The whole class was interested in exploring animals and nature, with a concentration on dinosaurs. With this learner-driven focus in mind, I set out to plan a four-week-long exploration of dinosaurs.

Think: Seeking Knowledge from Resources and Each Other

Learners started by exploring various fiction and nonfiction books about dinosaurs in a whole-class setting. When listening to the books, learners were instructed to use the "connection" sign. When I shared a book or resource and a learner had a connection with information in the book or resource, such as a fact the learner already knew, the learner would use the connection sign. In this silent share tech-nique, learners point their thumb and pinky finger out, fold down their three middle fingers, and then shake their hand back and forth while pointing at themselves and the educator. This symbol is translated as "me too" in American Sign Language and is a way for learners to share a connection while allowing the book and resource sharing to continue. This technique allows learners to communicate connections while still listening and focusing on the task at hand and collecting knowledge and information. The "connection" sharing process also is a way of setting group norms and is one way that learners can share connections with materials in a collaborative group setting.

Grow: Building on Knowledge to Develop Questions

After the sharing of fiction and nonfiction books, kindergarteners participated in a whole-class share-out of information they learned about dinosaurs from the mate-rials. The information was documented on a board in the school library. This was a way for learners to share information and build knowledge with other learners. They were also listening to other learners in a group setting and making connections to share their own understandings and questions.

Next, learners expressed interest in learning more about specific types of dino-saurs and brainstormed questions for which they would like to seek answers. The process was a way for learners to make connections with their existing knowledge

TABLE 6.1 /
Collaborate learning trajectory: PreSchool–second grade

Think

"Inquire, think critically, and gain knowledge. This is a cognitive domain." (AASL 2018, 15)

Create

"Draw conclusions, make informed decisions, apply knowledge to new situations, and create new knowledge. This is a psychomotor domain." (AASL 2018, 15)

"Learners identify collaborative opportunities by":

Learner III.A.1

"Demonstrating their desire to broaden and deepen understandings."

Learners will be able to:

- Articulate subject areas they are interested in as they explore fiction and nonfiction books
- Formulate questions based on the readings shared
- Make connections with existing knowledge on a topic and formulate questions
- Express their understanding orally or visually
- Pursue an area of interest within a topic to explore more deeply

Learner III.A.2

"Developing new understandings through engagement in a learning group."

Learners will be able to:

- Cite proof in words or images to illustrate their understanding of a text shared
- Listen to another learner, make connections with that learner's thinking, and build on it

Learner III.A.3

"Deciding to solve problems informed by group interaction."

Learners will be able to:

- Identify challenges in material
- Brainstorm, in small-group and whole class settings, solutions to problems
- Make connections to problems identified in readings with their world and the world around them
- Prototype solutions to problems identified in small group or whole class settings

"Learners participate in personal, social, and intellectual networks by":

Learner III.B.1

"Using a variety of communication tools and resources."

Learners will be able to:

- Make their thinking visible using written, visual, oral, digital and building tools
- Participate in small- and large-group sharing and question generating
- Work in small groups to plan and build with others to express understanding

Learner III.B.2

"Establishing connections with other learners to build on their own prior knowledge and create new knowledge."

Learners will be able to:

- Brainstorm with others to make connections with material
- Make connections with others to develop a deeper understanding of the material
- Make connections with others to formulate deeper questions about the material

Share "Share knowledge and participate ethically and productively as members of our democratic society. The is an affective domain." (AASL 2018, 15)	**Grow** "Pursue personal and aesthetic growth. This is a developmental domain." (AASL 2018, 15)
"Learners work productively with others to solve problems by":	"Learners actively participate with others in learning situations by":

Share

"Learners work productively with others to solve problems by":

Learner III.C.1

"Soliciting and responding to feedback from others."

Learners will be able to:

- Be open to and listen to feedback from other learners and educators to inform their learning
- Provide constructive feedback to other learners based on concrete evidence

Learner III.C.2

"Involving diverse perspectives in their own inquiry processes."

Learners will be able to:

- Understand that multiple perspectives are needed to be an informed learner
- Understand that the school librarian is sharing several resources in order to have diverse perspectives
- Make edits and changes to a process or project based on feedback

Grow

"Learners actively participate with others in learning situations by":

Learner III.D.1

"Actively contributing to group discussions."

Learners will be able to:

- Participate in whole-class sharing of connections and ideas
- Brainstorm ideas in small- and large-group settings
- Make connections with other learners by listening and adding to the discussion
- Follow group norms for small- and large-group work
- Identify ways to compromise and resolve conflict while engaged in group work

Learner III.D.2

"Recognizing learning as a social responsibility."

Learners will be able to:

- Plan, design, and build a solution in small groups to solve a problem identified in the inquiry process
- Share their work with the school community, including other grade levels, administration, and parents

Source: Created by Mary Catherine Coleman for the Francis W. Parker School Library, Chicago, Illinois.

about the topic and determine questions they wanted to answer. They were also collaborating with other learners to generate questions. Learners were placed in small groups based on the type of dinosaur they were most interested in exploring. This grouping allowed kindergarteners to pursue an area of interest within a topic of study.

Kindergarteners had a list of questions to answer based on the brainstorming session. Learners listened to online database articles to answer questions. They also explored nonfiction books with educators to find answers to their questions. Learners dictated information they found to educators, citing proof from the articles to illustrate their understanding. In addition, by using print and online databases for research, kindergarteners were learning about different materials they can use to gain information and different perspectives.

Create: Working Together to Illustrate Knowledge and Understanding

Next, kindergarteners were presented with their building challenge: using the information they collected about their dinosaur, including habitat, food sources, predators, and prey, as a class they had to build "Dinosaur Island" to illustrate the habitat their dinosaur would live in and what other dinosaurs would share its habitat. Kindergarteners used different kinds of building materials, including construction paper, clay, pipe cleaners, and the like, to illustrate what they learned about their dinosaur. A set of plastic dinosaurs of different species was purchased at a dollar store for each group to include in its habitat. Then each small group worked collaboratively with other groups to map out "Dinosaur Island," determining where the different habitats would go and the space for each dinosaur habitat. Learners had to work and compromise in small groups to illustrate the information they had learned. They made their thinking visible with different building materials and negotiated and collaborated with their partners to design and plan their habitat.

Throughout the process, when conflict arose between learners, the classroom educators or I would sit with the learners and talk through the challenges to reach a compromise. This was a way to model negotiation and compromise strategies for learners. Kindergarteners also needed to compromise and work with other classmates to design and plan the larger "Dinosaur Island." Learners listened to each other, provided feedback about each group's habitats, and made compromises and redesigned to build an island that reflected their knowledge and understanding of dinosaurs.

Share: Sharing Thinking and Knowledge with Others

At the end of the unit, each group shared its dinosaur's habitat and explained its design. Kindergarteners shared facts about their species of dinosaur, and educators typed up the information. "Dinosaur Island" and information sheets were displayed in the school library for other classes and grade levels to explore. The young learners were excited to see their work on display and to share their knowledge with learners outside their class and grade level.

COLLABORATIVE MINDSET: THIRD–FIFTH GRADES

As learners move into the third grade from early elementary school, they should be moving into more-advanced forms of collaboration as well. The foundation that they have developed in their earlier school years provides a solid introduction to the ideas of collaboration and gives them strategies to help navigate learning with and from each other. The collaboration goals in this next phase should focus on strengthening those skills, continuing to give learners time and space to cultivate their collaborative skills, along with the introduction of more independent and learner-led opportunities so learners feel more empowered as collaborators. Similar to the trajectory of the preschool through second-grade years, learners in third through fifth grades will need time and space to collaborate with peers, including room for conflict, negotiation, and compromise (table 6.2). They will need to be redirected when they encounter challenges in collaboration with other learners, both in small groups and in whole-class situations. By the time learners move out of the intermediate school grades, they will have advanced on the collaboration trajectory, be aware of the benefits of learning from others, and be more aware of themselves and their interactions in a collaborative environment.

Collaborate in Action: Overcoming Obstacles

The fifth-grade learners at my school focus on the theme of overcoming obstacles and challenges. This theme is woven into the curriculum in the book that they read, *The Knight in Rusty Armor* by Robert Fisher. The book is the story of a knight who must follow the path of truth to discover more about himself. Along the way he has help from several new friends as he learns to overcome challenges and become his best self. This book is taught in the lead-up to a four-day camping trip. For many of the fifth graders, this is the first time they have spent significant time in nature, away from family, and sharing cabins. Throughout the camping trip, learners make connections between the themes of the book and what they are experiencing as they hike, take on building challenges, and navigate the social aspects of sharing living space with their classmates for several days. The fifth graders keep journals to document their experiences on the trip.

I collaborated with the fifth-grade educators to design a project for learners to think about the themes identified in the book, their experiences on the camping trip, and what they learned about working with others. The plan was for fifth graders to work in small groups to build and design a working pinball machine that illustrated their understanding of the book and made connections with their personal experiences on the trip in collaboration with their partners. The pinball machines' games would tell a story in the details and the designs of the background and the

TABLE 6.2 /
Collaborate learning trajectory: Third–fifth grades

Think

"Inquire, think critically, and gain knowledge. This is a cognitive domain." (AASL 2018, 15)

"Learners identify collaborative opportunities by":

Learner III.A.1

"Demonstrating their desire to broaden and deepen understandings."

Learners will be able to:

- Make connections with information and knowledge shared in materials and by fellow learners.
- Develop deep-dive questions about a topic. (Deep-dive questions make connections to background knowledge; knowledge needs to be inferred, and a text does not give the learner the answer.)
- Seek answers to questions from multiple types of resources
- Work with others to explore resources and materials, develop questions, and plan the process to seek information.
- Identify an area of interest within a topic to explore more deeply.

Learner III.A.2

"Developing new understandings through engagement in a learning group."

Learners will be able to:

- Engage in thinking routines with other learners that include sharing their connections and listening to other learners to make deeper connections
- Listen to other learners and develop questions based on connections and ideas shared

Learner III.A.3

"Deciding to solve problems informed by group interaction."

Learners will be able to:

- Collect data from resources and identify problems based on research collected
- Prototype solutions to problems identified
- Redesign prototype solutions when initial iteration does not work
- Communicate their own ideas, listen to the ideas of other learners, and negotiate a collaborative solution to share

Create

"Draw conclusions, make informed decisions, apply knowledge to new situations, and create new knowledge. This is a psychomotor domain." (AASL 2018, 15)

"Learners participate in personal, social, and intellectual networks by":

Learner III.B.1

"Using a variety of communication tools and resources."

Learners will be able to:

- Expand their abilities to communicate orally with other learners
- Expand their abilities to make their thinking visible through building and constructing to illustrate knowledge
- Expand their use of resources to include print, databases, and websites to find information
- Develop skills to communicate online with others
- Develop their understanding of social media as a digital resource

Learner III.B.2

"Establishing connections with other learners to build on their own prior knowledge and create new knowledge."

Learners will be able to:

- Organize collaborative work with other learners to complete a project expressing the new knowledge created
- Use a variety of communication tools to connect with other learners

Share	**Grow**
"Share knowledge and participate ethically and productively as members of our democratic society. This is an affective domain." (AASL 2018, 15)	"Pursue personal and aesthetic growth. This is a developmental domain." (AASL 2018, 15)
"Learners work productively with others to solve problems by":	"Learners actively participate with others in learning situations by":
Learner III.C.1	**Learner III.D.1**
"Soliciting and responding to feedback from others."	"Actively contributing to group discussions."
Learners will be able to:	Learners will be able to:
• Listen to and be open to feedback from other learners and educators to inform their learning • Respond to feedback on their work with thoughtful questions and reflections on their own work • Provide constructive feedback to other learners offering proof in the work to support their thoughts • Begin to provide constructive feedback in a digital setting as well as in person	• Participate in whole-class sharing of connections and ideas • Share connections and knowledge in small-group settings • Work with others in small groups to create and share collective understandings of knowledge and ideas
Learner III.C.2	**Learner III.D.2**
"Involving diverse perspectives in their own inquiry processes."	"Recognizing learning as a social responsibility."
Learners will be able to:	Learners will be able to:
• Continue to expand their understanding that multiple perspectives are needed to be an informed learner • Begin to recognize when voices are missing from information seeking • Begin to plan their own inquiry path and rethink their path when they encounter roadblocks • Seek assistance from other learners or educators when they encounter challenges in the inquiry process • Use strategies to compromise and communicate with others including setting group norms to manage the collaborative process	• Start to recognize their strengths and challenges in collaborative work with others • Engage in the self-reflection process to better understand how they work with others • Approach the reflection process from the "I" perspective, reflecting on their role in the collaborative process and not that of other learners

Source: Created by Mary Catherine Coleman for the Francis W. Parker School Library, Chicago, Illinois.

obstacles. Learners also needed to think about how the path of the ball expressed the experience of the challenges.

The goal of a pinball machine is to keep the ball on the board for as long as possible to earn the most points. Learners needed to think about that objective as they designed their games and made connections either with the challenges the knight in the book experienced or the challenges they experienced on the camping trip. For example, one group thought about how hard it was to start a fire on their camping trip. They designed one path on their pinball board whereby, when a player hit the ball, the ball would shoot to the top of the board and roll back down the middle, making it impossible to hit the ball with the flippers of the pinball machine, thus ending the game. This path represented not overcoming challenges. However, if the player hit the ball at a different, more challenging angle, the ball would go up a small ramp, hit a button that caused a light to go on, and bounce off obstacles at an angle that allowed the player to hit it with the flippers. On this path, hitting the button to cause the light to go on represented overcoming the challenge of lighting the fire, and allowing the ball to stay in play kept the game going, also representing overcoming challenges. The goals of the project were for learners to make visible their thinking about and understanding of the literature, make connections with their own experiences, plan and follow the instructions to build the base model of their pinball machines, and then work with partners to plan, design, and build a working machine that told a story about their understanding of overcoming challenges.

Share: Collaborating to Build a Working Machine

The first step was to build the machines. The fifth-grade team of educators and I were able to purchase cardboard pinball machine kits. The learners worked in groups of three during this project. Fifth graders found information from a variety of sources: looking at all the materials provided in the kit, reading the written directions, and watching the assembly video. They needed to plan and work together to map out the process, decide who was going to do what in the process, and map out their plan to ensure that they completed the process in the time given to build their base machine. When learners encountered challenges, they had to talk to each other and rethink their process. Groups that struggled to complete a step in the design process turned to other groups for assistance. Learners were learning from different resources, from their collaborative partners, and from other classmates to complete this process.

Think: Making Deep Connections with Other Learners

When the learners finished building the base model, they started designing and planning their game. First, the fifth-grade team and I shared videos of pinball machines and talked about the themes and stories of challenges that the games were telling. Learners shared ideas in whole-class discussions about what they noticed about the games and how the illustrations, placement of the bumpers in the games, and obstacles in the ball's path all contributed to telling a story. The first task learners were given was to work in their collaborative groups and, in three to five sentences, write the story that their machine was going to tell. To write a short story, the fifth graders made connections with themes from the book, looked through their journals from the camping trip, and talked to their partners as they thought about challenges and experiences from the trip. They compromised and negotiated during this process to ensure that all the pieces of the pinball machine connected to their camping trip or the book and that each learner's experience and ideas were incorporated into the game.

Next, they mapped out the design of the machine, including materials they would make and build, where they would place obstacles, and the connections of their design to the story. Learners had access to all the materials in the school library's makerspace, including fabric, paint, and clay as well as the 3-D printers, a laser cutter, and simple circuits.

Then learners discussed what jobs each member of the team would do to complete their machines, who was going to build what, and how they were going to complete their plan. Learners discussed with each other their own personal strengths and interests and how they would contribute to the group project.

Create and Share:
Designing, Giving and Receiving Feedback, and Redesigning Together

Throughout the building process, learners encountered challenges. Sometimes their original design plan did not turn out the way they had intended, and they had to discuss with their group how they would rethink and redesign different elements. Using website searches and online videos, the fifth graders researched different ways to incorporate various materials, including using simple circuits to add lights and sound to their machines. This process included many iterations of building and testing to get the circuits to work the way the group planned. The learners sought feedback from other groups by asking them to test the machines and see if the games were enjoyable. The fifth-grade educators and I facilitated the process, offering advice, helping to negotiate conflict, listening to challenges, and researching resources with learners.

Think and Grow: Reflecting and Assessing

The fifth-grade team of educators and I were assessing and reflecting on the learners' process throughout the project to document process and progress. Most of the assessment happened in conversations with learners, talking to groups about their process and plans. The fifth graders shared their plans and explained how those plans connected with the literature, their experiences on the camping trip, and their journal writings, offering evidence for their thinking. As groups planned their machines, they shared how each element of the project connected to the deeper theme of over-coming challenges and obstacles. Fifth graders were also given prompts to reflect on the collaborative process, talking about challenges their groups encountered and how learners were able to overcome those challenges or whether they needed the assistance of an educator to help negotiate a compromise. These conversations and observations were collected so that the team of educators could reflect on the proj-ect and think about what we would do differently next time. For the learners, the documentation and observations were an assessment of their understanding of the literature, connections to the themes in the book and to their personal experiences on the camping trip, and their strengths and challenges in collaborative work.

COLLABORATIVE MINDSET: SIXTH-EIGHTH GRADES

By middle school, learners should be adept at all the collaboration skills mapped out in the earlier elementary school years. In the middle school years, learners should be comfortable learning and sharing with each other in large-group settings and should have spent time in collaborative small-group work in which they were empowered to plan and design with other learners. They also should have been given opportunities to determine group norms for collaborative groups, encoun-tered conflict, and worked on strategies to help resolve issues. Learners should have spent time working on their listening skills and developing strategies to engage with other learners to build and add to knowledge and information shared by peers. For these learners, self-reflection has become a routine part of the collaborative process, with many opportunities to think about their work and interactions in collaborative groups and to take note of positive results and challenges. From that self-reflection, middle school learners have become better than younger learners at knowing what group norms they need to be successful collaborators, as well as recognizing that other learners will need to be able to have a say in those group norms so that the whole group can be successful. This ability to empathize, read, and work with others should be a focus in the middle school years. As learners move into middle school, the opportunities for collaboration should continue to grow, and learners should be given more opportunities to take ownership of the process and projects (table 6.3).

Collaborate in Action: National Novel Writing Month

National Novel Writing Month (NaNoWriMo 2019) is a nonprofit organization that focuses on inspiring creativity and encouraging writing. Each November writers can sign up on the platform and commit to writing fifty thousand words by the end of the month. All writers—from published authors to those with just a spark of an idea—can participate in the program.

NaNoWriMo also provides a young writers platform by means of which educa-tors can engage their learners in the process (https://ywp.nanowrimo.org/pages/for-educators). The educators' program allows them to sign up learners in a secure digital forum where participants can commit to producing a specific number of words in the month and then write and share their work with peers. Educators can offer edits to learners' work. For the past three years, Annette Lesak, a middle and upper school librarian, and Eric Rampson, a library staff member and published author, have offered a NaNoWriMo program for middle school learners.

Connecting to the Curriculum and Learner Interest

The middle school English curriculum involves learners in expressing themselves and sharing their ideas and understanding through creative writing opportunities. In addition to studying the published works of a diverse collection of authors, learners are tasked with sharing their thoughts, ideas, and understandings through creative writing in journals, short stories, and other formats. The pair of educators connected with the English Department to offer NaNoWriMo as an opportunity for learners to pursue their own writing, interests, and passions while fulfilling creative writing assignments from their English educators.

Each October, in anticipation of the start of NaNoWriMo in November, Lesak and Rampson visit English department classes so the sixth through eighth graders can learn about the program. Learners who decide to participate are added to the secure digital platform by the two school library staffers and are given access to the online platform.

As added incentive to participate, along with the writing counting toward English class assignments, learners are told that anyone who completes a book of more than five thousand words will have that book published and added to the school library's collection.

Think and Create:
Making Individual Work Collaborative during NaNoWriMo

The first meeting of the learners includes an explanation of the month and how the program works. Learners plan and outline their work. They are free to choose any format, from poetry to a graphic novel. Learners set their own timelines for accomplishing the challenge. Next, the school library team members share the group norms for online conversations through the NaNoWriMo platform, and all participants agree to follow the norms of the digital communication. The website is open only to those learners participating because it is a space to ask questions and seek feedback when participants need advice about a challenge in their writing and because it is a place for encouragement and support.

Throughout the month, learners work on their projects and attend write-ins during lunchtime once a week. During these sessions, the school library staff members engage learners in writers' routines and give learners challenges to help them make progress in their own writing. Some of the challenges include using random words in a quick writing challenge, writing a short introduction to a book about a

TABLE 6.3 /
Collaborate learning trajectory: Sixth–eighth grades

Think "Inquire, think critically, and gain knowledge. This is a cognitive domain." (AASL 2018, 15)	**Create** "Draw conclusions, make informed decisions, apply knowledge to new situations, and create new knowledge. This is a psychomotor domain." (AASL 2018, 15)
"Learners identify collaborative opportunities by":	"Learners participate in personal, social, and intellectual networks by":

Learner III.A.1

"Demonstrating their desire to broaden and deepen understandings."

Learners will be able to:

- Map out and plan their own inquiry process
- Document their questions and research path based on a framework provided by educators
- Express their interests to pursue inquiry on a topic within a subject area

Learner III.A.2

"Developing new understandings through engagement in a learning group."

Learners will be able to:

- Engage with other learners to share their connections and listen to other learners to include the perpectives of others in the inquiry process
- Communicate in person and digitally with other learners to advance their inquiry process

Learner III.A.3

"Deciding to solve problems informed by group interaction."

Learners will be able to:

- Identify problems in the inquiry process both as individuals and in small- and large-group settings
- Begin to use processes like design thinking (outlined in chapter 4) to gain empathy and understanding for others to define problems

Learner III.B.1

"Using a variety of communication tools and resources."

Learners will be able to:

- Continue to expand their abilities to communicate orally with other learners
- Continue to expand their abilities to make their thinking visible through building and constructing to illustrate knowledge
- Begin to become multiliterate using different resources and tools to communicate, including visual, audio, and illustrations, as well as making and creating in print and digitally

Learner III.B.2

"Establishing connections with other learners to build on their own prior knowledge and create new knowledge."

Learners will be able to:

- Express and communicate their ideas and knowledge in small- and large-group settings
- Make connections with the perspectives and ideas of their peers to grow their knowledge
- Express connections with other learners in person and in digital formats
- Manage and organize the inquiry process documenting prior knowledge and including new knowledge learned in whole-class discussions and in small-group and individual research

Share

"Share knowledge and participate ethically and productively as members of our democratic society. This is an affective domain." (AASL 2018, 15)

Grow

"Pursue personal and aesthetic growth. This is a developmental domain." (AASL 2018, 15)

"Learners work productively with others to solve problems by":	"Learners actively participate with others in learning situations by":
Learner III.C.1	**Learner III.D.1**
"Soliciting and responding to feedback from others."	"Actively contributing to group discussions."
Learners will be able to:	Learners will be able to:
• Share work, receive feedback from educators and peers, and use that feedback to redesign their work, reflecting the new perspectives • Go through multiple iterations of a project • Give constructive feedback to other learners, including providing evidence for their thinking and being able to ask informed questions in order to provide meaningful feedback	• Begin to recognize their own learning styles and needs in group dynamics, as well as those of other learners • Begin to recognize the feelings and emotions of collaborative partners and navigate group dynamics • Map and plan collaborative projects, including setting group norms, sharing ideas, and determining division of labor • Be equipped with negotiation skills and plans to resolve conflict with other learners
Learner III.C.2	**Learner III.D.2**
"Involving diverse perspectives in their own inquiry processes."	"Recognizing learning as a social responsibility."
Learners will be able to:	Learners will be able to:
• Recognize why having diverse perspectives is important to the inquiry and collaborative processes • Organize and map their inquiry process and recognize what perspectives and points of view are important to include • Map the system of their inquiry process, recognize when and whose voices are missing, and determine how to seek them out and include them	• Recognize the contributions of collaborative partners and articulate what each group member brought to the learning experience and what they learned from other learners • Reflect on their own process and document the collaborative process and their engagement with other learners • Articulate the benefits of a collaborative process or the negative interactions and what they learned from these interactions

Source: Created by Mary Catherine Coleman for the Francis W. Parker School Library, Chicago, Illinois.

random character, or completing a rapid writing challenge (writing a one-hundred-word story in three minutes using random words shouted out by the group). During these write-ins, middle schoolers share the work they have done, receive feedback, and offer ideas and encouragement to other learners. Lesak and Rampson also offer ideas and assistance to learners as they work through challenges, need research or background knowledge for their books, or work through writer's block. In the online forum, monitored by the school librarians, participants learn to communicate with each other and offer and receive feedback in a digital setting.

Share and Grow:
Reworking, Giving and Receiving Feedback, and Sharing

During the month, middle schoolers document their work, follow the timeline, read their fellow writers work, help each other overcome challenges with their writing, and offer suggestions about the story lines, characters, or plots of their classmates' books. Participants learn how to offer constructive feedback and honor and respect the work that other learners put into their writing because they are going through the same process. Middle schoolers learn more about themselves and each other as they share their writing, learning what constructive feedback is, how to deliver suggestions that are helpful, and how to incorporate feedback into their work. Learners share with each other and the school library staff ways that collaboration and feedback during the process help them in their writing.

After learners finish writing their books, editing them, and incorporating suggestions from educators and other learners, they design the cover for their books and submit the final product. The school library staffers use an online publishing service to have the works printed. The final books are added to the library collection and shared in a public book display in the school library. Middle schoolers are excited and proud to have their books published and shared in the school library for other community members to check out. This process is a passion- and interest-driven experience for the middle schoolers, makes connections with the English department's curricular goals, and engages learners in a collaborative process in which they learn how to be empathetic collaborators.

COLLABORATIVE MINDSET: NINTH–TWELFTH GRADES

As learners advance into the high school years, their collaboration skills should continue to grow and extend beyond the walls of the school (table 6.4). Learners should be skilled at seeking resources and materials in print and digital formats. They should already know how to organize, plan, and set group norms for collaborative partnerships. Learners should also have internalized a set of routines for giving and receiving feedback in collaborative groups and be regularly incorporating and integrating feedback into individual and group work. The essential process refinements in collaboration in the high school years include moving beyond the school walls to collaborate with others to seek information, present work, and receive feedback. Learners should be given many opportunities to receive feedback on their work from authentic sources so that learners understand how to work and collaborate with others outside the comfort of a school community.

An authentic audience also adds more meaning and purpose to learners' work by providing real-world meaning and impact to the outcomes. When learners work with individuals and groups outside the school setting, they have opportunities to make deeper connections by applying their work to an actual problem, issue, or concept present in the world. They also have a chance to learn more about being flexible when working with other individuals and personalities who are not peers but individuals who do not know them on a personal or social level, an important component of advancing as a collaborator.

Collaborate in Action: Social Entrepreneurship

The school librarian teaches a social entrepreneurship class for high school learners. The focus of the class is on engaging learners in the entrepreneurship process with local businesses that also have a social justice or community service mission. One goal of the elective is for learners to learn more about all aspects of a start-up business and the challenges that entrepreneurs face as they build their businesses, from financing to hiring practices to building a customer base. An additional goal for the class is that learners immerse themselves in the social justice issues to which the company is committed. This educator partners with a local business in Chicago that is engaged in social entrepreneur work. Learners work with a business consultant to learn more about what it takes to get funding and navigate the legal paperwork needed to start a business. The class learns about the mission and practices of the business and how those connect to the social justice movement to which the business is committed. Learners spend time with the owners of the business and hear about some of the challenges that they are facing, and then learners are asked to come up with solutions for a problem the business faces. The high schoolers work on their ideas and plans in whole-class and small-group collaborations and present their solutions to the business owners to not only offer tangible solutions to real-world problems but also learn how to receive authentic feedback from the business owners, to listen to the feedback, and to integrate it into their plans.

Engaging with a Real-World Challenge: Back of the Yards Coffee Co.

Back of the Yards Coffee Co. is a coffeehouse in the Back of the Yards neighborhood in Chicago. The neighborhood has a challenging history of racial and social inequity. These systemic issues have resulted in a lack of economic growth and a rise in gang violence. The founders of the coffeehouse grew up in the neighborhood and are committed to creating a community space and elevating the neighborhood through the shop. The mission of Back of the Yards Coffee Co. is to bring well-

TABLE 6.4 /
Collaborate learning trajectory: Ninth–twelfth grades

Think "Inquire, think critically,and gain knowledge. This is a cognitive domain." (AASL 2018, 15)	**Create** "Draw conclusions, make informed decisions, apply knowledge to new situations, and create new knowledge. This is a psychomotor domain." (AASL 2018, 15)
"Learners identify collaborative opportunities by":	"Learners participate in personal, social, and intellectual networks by":

Think (continued)

"Learners identify collaborative opportunities by":

Learner III.A.1

"Demonstrating their desire to broaden and deepen understandings."

Learners will be able to:

- Map out and plan their inquiry process
- Explain the goals and outcomes they have set for their inquiry process
- Take a topic or subject and map out the systems and connections, deepening their understandings and documenting their inquiry process

Learner III.A.2

"Developing new understandings through engagement in a learning group."

Learners will be able to:

- Find and collect information from print and digital resources, as well as engage with experts and individuals outside the school community to deepen understandings
- Communicate in person and in digital environments to share perspectives and ideas
- Engage in digital communications with individuals outside the school community, understanding how to craft questions for experts and how to reach out to them

Learner III.A.3

"Deciding to solve problems informed by group interaction."

Learners will be able to:

- Identify problems in the inquiry process both as individuals and in small- and large-group settings
- Identify problems in the inquiry process, in small-group and whole-class settings, that connect with the larger global world

Create (continued)

"Learners participate in personal, social, and intellectual networks by":

Learner III.B.1

"Using a variety of communication tools and resources."

Learners will be able to:

- Be multiliterate, using different resources and tools to communicate, including written, audio, and visual, as well as by making and creating in print and digital formats
- Process information from a variety of resources to collect data and share their understanding
- Share their thinking in different formats
- Move from processing information in these different formats to creating and producing information and new knowledge

Learner III.B.2

"Establishing connections with other learners to build on their own prior knowledge and create new knowledge."

Learners will be able to:

- Make connections with the perspectives and ideas of their peers, in small-group and whole-class settings, to grow their own knowledge
- Manage and organize the inquiry process, documenting their prior knowledge and including new knowledge learned in whole-class discussions, small-group work, and individual research
- Connect with individuals and organizations outside the school community to build new knowledge
- Recognize the different personalities of collaborative partners and adjust their discussion and interactions to meet different audiences

Share "Share knowledge and participate ethically and productively as members of our democratic society. This is an affective domain." (AASL 2018, 15)	**Grow** "Pursue personal and aesthetic growth. This is a developmental domain." (AASL 2018, 15)
"Learners work productively with others to solve problems by":	"Learners actively participate with others in learning situations by":

Share (continued)

"Learners work productively with others to solve problems by":

Learner III.C.1

"Soliciting and responding to feedback from others."

Learners will be able to:

- Share work and receive feedback from educators, peers, and an authentic audience
- Go through multiple iterations of a project
- Share their work beyond the school community with knowledge experts to receive authentic feedback in a real-world context
- Ask informed questions to provide meaningful feedback
- Give constructive feedback to peers, including providing evidence for their thinking and response

Learner III.C.2

"Involving diverse perspectives in their own inquiry processes."

Learners will be able to:

- Recognize that having diverse perspectives is important to the inquiry process and explain why
- Organize and map their inquiry process and recognize what perspectives and points of view are important to include
- Map the system of their inquiry process, recognize when and whose voices and perspectives are missing, and determine how to seek them out and include them

Grow (continued)

"Learners actively participate with others in learning situations by":

Learner III.D.1

"Actively contributing to group discussions."

Learners will be able to:

- Recognize their own learning style and respond to the different personalities of authentic audiences and individuals
- Recognize the feelings and emotions of collaborative partners, both inside and outside the school community, and navigate group dynamics
- Map and plan collaborative projects, including setting group norms, sharing ideas, and determining the division of labor
- Use their negotiation skills to resolve conflict with other learners

Learner III.D.2

"Recognizing learning as a social responsibility."

Learners will be able to:

- Recognize the contributions of collaborative partners and articulate what each group member brought to the learning experience and what they learned from each other
- Understand how they work best in collaborative partnerships and recognize the need to discuss personalities and work processes of other members of a collaborative group to set group norms and navigate the process of working together

Source: Created by Mary Catherine Coleman for the Francis W. Parker School Library, Chicago, Illinois.

paying jobs to the neighborhood, provide funds for scholarships and grants to young people by donating a portion of the profits, and purchase baked goods and materials from other local companies to spread economic growth. To be environmentally sustainable, the business composts 95 percent of its waste and has a relationship with the coffee bean source to ensure that the grower's workers receive a fair wage. The high school educator connected with the coffeehouse to work with her social entrepreneurship learners.

Think: Turning One-Time Customers into Repeat Customers

The owners of Back of the Yards Coffee Co. were struggling with how to turn one-time drop-in customers into repeat customers. The classroom educator and the company founders presented this challenge to the learners. The high schoolers spent time making connections between what they had learned about the running of a small business and the challenges facing the coffeehouse. They mapped the business system, highlighting the specific issues facing Back of the Yards Coffee Co. and the systemic social issues facing the neighborhood.

To better understand the business, members of the class brainstormed questions to use when gathering data from the company. The high schoolers collected information from the company owners, brainstormed questions based upon what they observed in the data, and worked with the class's business consultant to come up with solutions for challenges facing the company.

Learners also conducted research on coffeehouse culture. They interviewed and surveyed people in the school community to gather data on visits to coffee shops. The learners went out to coffeehouses in the area and observed and interviewed customers; they also visited Back of the Yards Coffee Co. to observe the customers and interview people in the neighborhood.

Create: Prototyping Solutions in Collaborative Groups

After the class members had collected their research and data, they brainstormed solutions to the problem. Learners worked in small groups to come up with different solutions and then pitched their favorites to the whole class. After the pitches had been made, the class members determined which solutions they wanted to work on and formed small working groups, each of which would focus on one solution. In the small groups, learners had to negotiate and work with each other, manage their time, map out the work that each member would do, and create their pitch to Back of the Yards Coffee Co.

The class's educator was a facilitator, working through challenges with different groups as they collaborated and compromised. By giving feedback to learners as they were creating their presentations, she also challenged the groups to make deeper connections or take ideas further.

Groups first shared their pitch presentations with the whole class and the business consultant to gather feedback and then had time to make changes and adjustments and rethink their pitch to incorporate constructive feedback and give constructive feedback to others.

Share and Grow: Offering Authentic Feedback for Real-World Challenges

For the final step of the project, each group of learners made their presentations to the owners of Back of the Yards Coffee Co., pitching the learners' ideas about how to make one-time customers into repeat customers. The pitches included the group's proposed solution, research behind and justification for their idea, and a plan for the implementation of their idea. One proposed solution was to create a mobile ordering system that connected to the company's existing purchasing software, thereby allowing customers to have a personal profile that would save their coffee preferences and suggest items based on their previous orders. Another group suggested a social media campaign called "From Crop to Cup" that shared the story of the coffee process and interviews with the employees involved in the process as well as the connections to people in the neighborhood who are employed by the company and receive the scholarship funds. The group felt that customers would be more committed to returning if they had a human connection to the company. Other ideas included a rewards program and a special sale for various groups of customers on different days of the week. The Back of the Yards Coffee Co. owners provided authentic feedback to the learners after their presentations. They commented on what would work but also reflected on what was not possible and why. This feedback gave the learners a window into the real-world challenges that businesses face.

This project allowed learners to engage in whole-class and small-group collaborations. The project required learners to collect data in a variety of ways and to define solutions to a real-world business problem. Learners were required to map out a variety of systems and understand the complexity of the intersection of these systems. Finally, throughout the process learners offered feedback to and received feedback from peers and experts and incorporated that feedback in their learning.

Reflecting on Learning across Grade Levels

Developing learning trajectories customized for individual learning communities allows school librarians to identify where their learners fall on the track. School librarians and other educators should take into account the unique context of their school community and curriculum and recognize that not all learners will reach development markers at the same time. School librarians should also be aware of the specific needs of their own community and recognize not only that learners are unique individuals but that each classroom, grade level, and school community is unique. School librarians should be aware of the intricacies of their school community as well as learners' needs and challenges outside the school setting, recognizing how these will affect the collaborative learning trajectory that learners follow.

Questions for the Reflective Practitioner

1. Where on the trajectory do I see the learners in my school? How might the development markers for my community differ from the example trajectory provided here?

2. What are ways that my school library or district can map the collaborative learning of my learners?

3. What can I and my school library department do to grow my learners' collaborative mindset through their educational experiences?

PART III

The School Library as the Center of Collaboration

7

Setting the Stage
for Collaboration

he National Building Museum in Washington, D.C., hosts a
five-week summer program for teenagers in the area called Investigating Where We Live. Thirty learners spend time exploring different
neighborhoods in the diverse city and then choosing a neighborhood
to focus on, curating photographs, interviews, writings, and their own observations
about the area ("Investigating Where We Live: Washington, DC" 2019). Then participants work with museum staff to curate an exhibit of the teens' work that expresses
their points of view. This project has been ongoing for more than twenty years and
highlights not only a shift in the ways that museums curate exhibits but also a changing idea about how visitors participate in their museum experience. In her book
The Participatory Museum, Nina Simon discussed the changing ideas and focus of
museums and the shift from traditional exhibit design in which the "institution provides content for visitors to consume" to the development of "experiences in which
visitors create, share, and connect with each other around content" (Simon 2010, 2).

In the example of the National Building Museum's Investigating Where We Live
project, the teenagers in the program are not just consuming information that has
been researched, selected, and designed by someone at the museum. Rather, teens
are given the opportunity to explore a neighborhood, observe, and think about the
history of that neighborhood and its place in the history of Washington, D.C. Then
they design the exhibit, selecting the images and information that were included in
the final share-out of the work. The participants are able to share their own artwork,
writings, and photographs to illustrate their point of view about the neighborhood.
They are not just consumers but creators of knowledge that is on public display. The
National Building Museum "provides the framework—the space, the sessions, the

instruction—but the content, design, and implementation of the exhibition are left up to the teenage participants" (Simon 2010, 233).

School libraries are going through similar shifts in visitor experiences. Libraries, once seen as the gatherers and keepers of knowledge to be consumed by learners, are now shifting to spaces and places where "learners actively participate" (AASL 2018, 87) and where "opportunities for sharing and collaboration by all members of the school community" exist (AASL 2018, 90). For school librarians to have an environment in which learners are welcomed not only to consume information and curate knowledge but also to collaborate and create new knowledge, the school library needs to be a physical space that is diverse and flexible to accommodate the varied needs of learners.

Creating a Space for Collaboration

The *National School Library Standards* state that the school library "provides a welcoming environment and facilitates programs that support inclusivity and diversity, encouraging participation by providing opportunities for sharing and collaboration by all members of the school community" (AASL 2018, 90). The curriculum of the school library is part of providing this environment, ensuring that there are deep connections to the mission and goals of the school and classroom curriculum. Working with other educators to make connections with the learning and the diverse needs of all learners in the school is another important element of this success. Keeping an up-to-date and diverse collection that reflects the members of the community and the diverse global world in which learners live, as well as resources in a variety of formats—both print and digital—to meet the information-seeking needs of learners is essential. These are all important aspects of creating a welcoming and inclusive environment in a school library.

Also important is the arrangement and use of the physical space. If school librarians are to facilitate "opportunities to integrate collaborative and shared learning" (AASL 2018, School Library III.A.) and support a culture of collaboration in the school library and the whole school, then the use of space in the school library must facilitate this type of learning. The school library space must offer learners not only the opportunity to interact with the information and with each other and to explore, to be hands-on, and to collaborate but also places for that collaboration to happen.

If the goals are for learners to retain information and to build on that knowledge, the design of the space is an essential part of reaching those goals. According to research in *The Third Teacher,* a resource that looks at the physical design of a space as an important element of learning, "research shows that people learn more deeply and retain knowledge longer when they have opportunities to engage actively with the information and experiences at hand" (O'Donnell Wicklund Pigozzi and Peterson 2010, 66).

A CHANGING SPACE I:
THE FRANCIS W. PARKER SCHOOL LIBRARY

Francis W. Parker School is located on the north side of Chicago, and it is land-locked. The school has been on the same spot for 117 years; the Lincoln Park neighborhood has grown up around the school and is one of the most densely populated neighborhoods in the city. Options did not exist for the footprint of the school building to grow up or out. As the school has grown, school leadership has had to be creative about how space is used in the existing building to meet the needs of the community. To remain relevant to learning, the school library has had to adjust and change and become more usable to justify occupying ten thousand square feet in a space-deficient building.

The school community wanted to rethink the school library curriculum and the space. The school library served about 950 learners and 200 faculty and staff. The school library had space and a generous budget, but the library was almost always empty. Learners did not use it. In 2014, Annette Lesak and I were hired to be the librarians at the school. When we joined the community, making the school library a more relevant space was one of our first charges. The school had a long-term fund-raising and renovation plan that was going to take about three years to complete. This time window between our arrival and the arrival of an architect and design team who would work with us and the community to redesign the space was an amazing opportunity for Lesak and me. We could play with the space by making small changes to see how learners really would use it. What we learned could then inform the best redesign of the space for their learning. Most important, we wanted to advance the curriculum to be more collaborative, and we wanted the school library space to facilitate opportunities for learners and educators to Think, Create, Share, and Grow. Lesak and I took several steps toward making those goals possible in the school library space.

Weeding Is Essential

First, Lesak and I weeded. The school library collection was estimated at more than ninety thousand print items when we started in the summer of 2014. Many of those books were out of date, were not relevant to the curriculum of the school, and did not meet the school's mission of being diverse, being inclusive of the members of the community, and reflecting the diverse world. Research shows that the visual environment can have a profound effect on the learning of children. A study published by the Association for Psychological Science found that "children were more distracted by the visual environment, spent more time off task, and demonstrated small learning gains when the walls were highly decorated than when the decorations were removed" (Fisher, Godwin, and Seltman 2014). That study focused on the wall decorations that were found in classrooms, but the same can be said of a cluttered library. We found that the plethora of books in the Parker collection made it harder for learners to find the materials and books they were looking for and that the crowded environment prevented learners from being able to use the space to collaborate and learn. The weeding opened up space so the school library could be a "learning environment that supports and stimulates discussion from all members of the school community" (AASL 2018, School Library III.D.1.). We spent almost a year weeding the collection, removing more than sixty-five thousand items. Books and resources that were still usable and relevant were donated to classroom libraries, other schools, and book donation organizations. Items that were inaccurate, were out of date, or contained offensive material were recycled and removed. As hard as throwing away books can be, sometimes that is the best and only choice for books that share ideas that are racist and factually inaccurate.

The weeding not only made the collection more accessible and usable for learners, it also freed up space. To make the school library more flexible and usable, the large, previously stuffed book stacks were dismantled and given to scrap metal collectors to be recycled. Dozens of book spin racks were donated to other school libraries around the city.

A Space for Everyone

Many school libraries function as a space in which various types of learning take place, from individual learning to whole-class learning to small-group collaboration. The school library can also be a comfortable space for learners to gather, read, listen to audiobooks and music, and socialize. The idea of flexible classrooms is growing in education. The University of Salford in the United Kingdom conducted an extensive study of the environmental factors that impact learner engagement and learning. Researchers looked at three factors of classroom design that had the largest impact on learning outcomes: naturalness (factors such as light and temperature), stimulation (factors such as color and visual complexity), and individualization (factors such as flexibility and learner ownership). The study found "clear evidence . . . that well-designed primary schools boost children's academic performance in reading, writing, and maths" (Barrett et al. 2015, 3). The study concluded that "well-defined and age appropriate learning zones are important to facilitate learning" (Barrett et al. 2015, 43) and that learning environments can "support individualization by offering a variety of opportunities for different modes of learning" (Barrett et al. 2015, 28). Part of the ability of the school library to support diverse learners is to offer flexible spaces that allow learners to choose the space that works best for their learning. This flexibility includes offering movable and different types of seating options throughout the school library in different learning zones so that learners have options about where and how to take advantage of the school library.

Flexible Seating

The next step for Lesak and me was to rethink the layout of the space to support a more diverse and usable space for all types of learning. Creating space by weeding the collection and getting rid of big, bolted-in-place bookcases allowed natural light to flow into the school library from the many windows. Also, because we had updated the old catalog system to a web-based system that could be searched from any smart device, more space became available when the outdated desktop computers and their tables were removed.

We wanted to use this open space to create zones in which learners could engage in their studies in different ways. We purchased bean bag chairs to spread out movable, comfy seating options throughout the space. A sofa, upholstered chairs, and a coffee table that had been discarded from an office created a social seating area for small-class discussions or for socializing. These new seating options that encouraged interactions among learners were part of "creating a learning environment in which learners understand that learning is a social responsibility" (AASL 2018, School Librarian III.D.2.).

The Power of Paint

The next focus was on low-cost tools for creativity and collaboration. We had visited a workspace in Chicago that had corkboard walls used to organize and share ideas. Corkboard was too expensive for our budget, but whiteboard paint would work to encourage collaborative work. With twenty-five dollars' worth of whiteboard paint purchased locally, our team painted table tops, the reference desk, and two walls in the space. The whiteboard spaces that invited learners to collaborate and share knowledge demonstrated and reinforced "the idea that information is a shared resource" (AASL 2018, School Library III.D.2.). The whiteboard spaces also "[stimulate] learners to actively contribute to group discussions" (AASL 2018, School Librarian III.D.1.).

A Space of Their Own

The University of Salford study mentioned previously found that individualization was key to a successful learning environment. The researchers found that when learners feel they have ownership in a space, they are more likely to be successful in that space and "that personalization of space is an important factor in the formation of an individual's identity and sense of self-worth" (Barrett et al. 2015, 30). In a shared space like a school library that can serve hundreds or, in some cases, thousands of learners, finding ways to give ownership to learners can be a challenge. Lesak and I sought ways to allow learners to have ownership and put their stamp on the school library space.

Learners Add Their Stamp

One of the school librarians hosted a "paint the bookends" party for middle school learners. Learners were invited to spend their lunch period in the school library painting the bookends. Dozens of middle schoolers came to the school library and painted the bookends with the cover art and characters from their favorite books to add personal touches to the bookshelves.

For the younger learners, I created a LEGO wall in the elementary school space. I purchased eighteen build plates, glued them to the wall, and then purchased bins of building bricks and got more as donations from school families. The LEGO wall became an ever-changing creation space in which learners, either before or after school, could make and build and add their creations to the wall. Learners' creations lasted several days until the pieces were needed for another learner's creation. Learners were able to gather and build together and share their designs and creativity—many times collaborating with learners from different classes or grade levels. The wall became an opportunity for learners to work with "diverse social and intellectual learner networks" (AASL 2018, School Library III.C.1.). The LEGOs and the wall also were used during classes' library time when they were integrated into learner research projects and were used to demonstrate connections to literature.

Learners were able to move tables, chairs, and bean bags around to suit what they were doing at the time. If a large group was gathering, learners could move the furniture to meet that need. If a learner wanted to take a bean bag chair to a quiet space in the school library to read alone, that was allowed. By giving learners some ownership to rearrange the space to meet their different learning needs, the school library became a space where learners wanted to be, a space they knew they could count on to help meet their needs.

The school library provided "a welcoming environment and [facilitated] programs that support inclusivity and diversity" (AASL 2018, 90). Ensuring that learners feel welcome and that the school library is a place for them to share their work and be able to learn in the way that is best for them is essential for the space to be welcoming and inclusive to all learners.

Putting Out the Welcome Mat

The other design challenge Lesak and I faced was the intimidating reference desk, which took up a large space, was awkward, and prevented comfortable interaction between staff members and school library users. The desk had been designed twenty years before and had many features that were no longer relevant, including room for a checkout card file and space for big, old desktop computers. We were inspired by the idea of genius bars at the Apple Store where customers can sit and talk to Apple employees about their devices. The lower part of the reference desk was painted with whiteboard paint to make a collaborative section for school librarians to work with learners who were looking for information. Chairs and bar stools added on both sides of the desk allowed learners and the school librarians to sit together. By creating a space for learners and educators to sit and talk with the school librarians and share ideas, we helped reinforce "the idea that information is a shared resource" (AASL 2018, School Library III.D.2.). The old card catalog drawers were transformed into planters for succulents, adding a warm, friendly touch to the reference desk.

These simple changes took what once was an intimidating, oversized barrier with much wasted space and turned it into a warm, welcoming spot where learners and educators enjoy gathering to discuss curriculum, to share books, or just to sit and socialize during the day. The small changes helped to redefine the whole atmosphere of the school library. Little things, such as the unintentional message being sent by a large, intimidating reference desk and how young learners or other educators might perceive it as a mandate to stay on the other side, can run counter to the environment that school librarians are trying to create in the school library. If a school library is to create "a learning environment that supports and stimulates discussion from all members of the school community" (AASL 2018, School Library III.D.1.), then the types and placement of furniture and the accessibility of the school library staff must convey that message.

Making the Redesign a Community Event

The three years during which the school library team was able to make small changes to the library space and to the curriculum were instrumental in gaining support of the school community for a large-scale renovation of the space. When the administrators, parents, and alumni were able to see how much more usable the space had become, how much more connected the curriculum in multiple disciplines could be, and how much more engaged learners were in the space, these stakeholders were supportive of financing a large-scale renovation of the school library.

During the design process for the new space, educators, learners, and parents were invited to design workshops in which they could share their ideas for the new space. This sharing had several benefits. It led many members of the school community to feel a sense of ownership in the new space, useful ideas were generated, and stakeholders felt that their voices were heard. Giving stakeholders opportunities to share their ideas was an important step in "consistently engaging with the school community to ensure that the school library resources, services, and standards align with the school's mission" (AASL 2018, School Library III.B.1.).

Lesak and I also incorporated what we had learned over the three years about how the space was used by learners and educators and the larger community. We wanted to get the best return possible on the investment in the large-scale renovation and ensure that the school library space was relevant and usable for everyone.

The renovated school library includes

- whiteboard tables, walls, and doors to encourage creation and collaboration;
- a LEGO table and a new makerspace that support learners' designing, proto-typing, and collaborating;
- individual study rooms as well as larger collaboration rooms and different types of seating throughout the space to meet the needs of all learners, whether they are working alone or in groups;
- all low bookcases (only three shelves each) to ensure that natural light flows through the space and that books are accessible to everyone, including learners and educators who use wheelchairs;
- wheels on all the bookcases so that the space can easily be reconfigured for grade-level and community events, making the space more usable to the community;
- seating designed to be usable by learners of all ages and heights, from pre-schoolers to high school seniors;
- tables that are height adjustable, so that all members of the school community feel like the whole space was designed for them—not just one side or one space;
- living green walls with plants to bring in natural elements (an idea proposed by learners); and
- a deck used by individual learners and by classes in good weather, giving learners even more options in their environment.

A major focus of the space was on flexibility and collaboration. Stakeholders wanted a school library environment in which learners could engage with materials and with each other. It was important that the space reflected the goals and mission of the school and ensured that learners "understand that learning is a social responsibility" (AASL 2018, School Librarian III.D.2.).

The mission of Parker is to ensure that learners understand what it means to be a citizen in a diverse world; being a part of a learning environment that is collaborative and social is an important part of developing that understanding. Therefore, everyone realized that the school library had to be a welcoming place that supported collaborating, learning, and sharing.

A CHANGING SPACE II: THE HUBBARD WOODS SCHOOL LIBRARY

At about the same time that changes were happening at the Francis W. Parker School library, not too far away, in the town of Winnetka, Illinois, the Hubbard Woods School library was experiencing similar issues. The neighborhood school is part of a suburban school district north of the city of Chicago. Most of the school buildings in the district are more than a century old, and many of the spaces have become outdated for current educational uses. Hubbard Woods is one of the district's elementary schools serving kindergarten through fourth grade. The building was one hundred years old, and the school library existed in what had been at one time the gymnasium. Forty years ago a new gym was built, and the school library took over the vacated space. The room was massive and beautiful with twenty-five-foot ceilings and arched windows. The space had beautiful brick walls and even a brick fireplace. Although the space was large and welcoming, it was not conducive to collaborative projects, STEM programs, and other uses by members of the school community. The challenge was the inflexibility of the space. It was designed in the older tradition of school libraries with heavy, large tables and bookcases bolted to the floor.

Todd Burleson became the school librarian after fourteen years as a classroom educator at the Hubbard Woods School. His first challenge was to create a more collaborative and active space for learners and the whole school community. The school district hoped that the changes made at the Hubbard Woods School would be a model for advancing and changing the school library spaces throughout the district.

Weeding Is Essential—Again

Burleson also weeded at the Hubbard Woods School library, opening up space for some of the environmental changes he envisioned but also allowing him to open up shelf space for new, more relevant books for learners. The school library had been weeded only sparingly over the years, resulting in materials that had not circulated in years, were no longer connected to the curriculum, did not reflect the diversity and complexity of the learners and the global community, and were not of interest to the learners. Burleson said, "I discovered the importance of weeding. An effective weeding program is essential to the health of a collection. Weed mercilessly and work diligently to get the collection to mirror the needs of learners and staff."

When the school library is current and effective, the space contributes to "creating and maintaining a learning environment that supports and stimulates discussion from all members of the school community" (AASL 2018, School Library III.D.1.). A weeding program is an essential aspect of maintaining a collaborative learning environment for the school community—an environment in which learners can collaborate as they Think, Create, Share, and Grow. Burleson went on to say, "Libraries must be living, breathing organisms, not static collections or museums. The collection must be able to breathe and grow."

Recasting a Space for Everyone

As Burleson and his principal were discussing options for the school library space at Hubbard Woods, the carpet was being replaced, and they decided that, instead of bolting the big bookcases back into the floor through the new carpet, they would seize the opportunity to make the space more inviting and flexible. Burleson and the school maintenance staff cut twelve-foot-long bookcases into three-foot sections, replaced the tops and bottoms of the shelving units, and added casters. The result was an entire school library that was movable without the need to purchase many new materials. The team had funds to replace the old, heavy wood tables with lighter, movable tables that flip up and nest to be stored compactly in a corner. New, ergonomically designed chairs that can be stacked and stored were also purchased. The whole space can be rearranged in a manner of minutes by a minimum number of staff. The school librarian stated, "The space gets entirely transformed from library to assembly hall at least once a week. The room literally adapts to the needs of the school." He also shared that the design of the space included different types of seating to meet different learner needs. Semipermanent spaces that encourage different types of collaboration between learners are found in the Hubbard Woods School library. Tables and nooks throughout the space allow learners to plan and organize their projects. The space also has soft spaces with cushions and comfortable seating for individual learners to relax, reflect, and process. The school library has large gathering spaces for whole-class and large-group discussion, brainstorming, and idea share-out. The school library space changes and meets the needs of the learners and the school community, making it the center of the school.

Centering on Learners' Passions

Making the Hubbard Woods School library a learner-centered space was essential to the school librarian. The flexibility of the large space and the tall ceilings support unique, collaborative experiences for learners. One example is the drone cage built by the school librarian so that learners can code and fly drones in the library space. He got the idea when he saw drone cages online for makerspaces. The cost of these systems was prohibitive, so the school librarian got creative. His research revealed several options, and he finally decided on a game called "9 Square in the Air" that was designed for physical education classes. The game comes with PVC pipes that connect, making it easy to assemble, disassemble, and store. Plus, the system could be shared with the physical education department to support that curriculum. The system was fitted with inexpensive deer fence netting to cover the piping and prevent the drones from "escaping" the cage. With some creativity and collaboration with another education department, the school librarian was able to use the library space to advance part of the school library curriculum and tap into a passion of his learners. The program engages learners in collaborative projects and "[demonstrates and reinforces] the idea that information is a shared resource" (AASL 2018, School Library III.D.2.).

Creating a Gathering Place

Burleson was focused on making the Hubbard Woods School library a welcoming space for his co-educators, as well as for learners, instead of a "shushing space." One of the simple, inexpensive changes he made was to create a charging station for educators to charge laptops, iPads, and phones. This station created a magnet spot for educators to hang out in the library, meet other educators, chat, and get to know each other better. Investing in a single-cup coffee machine attracted other educators to the school library and created another good spot for the school librarian and other educators to chat. More interactions among the educators led to a better sense of community in the school and established the school library as a place for all members of the school community. Burleson was able to create an environment in which educators felt welcomed and comfortable hanging out, which, in turn, opened opportunities to talk with other educators and make connections on personal and professional levels. The opportunity for educators to gather and talk about curriculum contributed to "facilitating diverse social and intellectual learner networks" (AASL 2018, School Library III.C.1.).

The school librarian set up an inexpensive monitor in the library and shared work and projects that learners had created in the school library space. When educators stopped by to recharge a phone or have a cup of coffee, they could see the work that other educators and learners were doing. This public display of their work pleased learners and gave educators ideas for projects that could be incorporated into their courses. Conversations among educators sparked new curricular connections across disciplines, leading to a more collaborative teaching and learning environment. A few simple changes and additions led to "creating and maintaining a learning environment that supports and stimulates discussion from all members of the school community" (AASL 2018, School Library III.D.1.). The welcoming environment that the school librarian cultivated for co-educators led to more collaborations between classroom educators and the school library and was achieved through simple changes that led to "partnering with other educators to scaffold learning and organize learner groups to broaden and deepen understanding" (AASL 2018, School Library III.A.1.).

Engaging the Community and Aligning Goals

Burleson engaged the Hubbard Woods School community in a variety of ways as the school library was redesigned and renovated and as it continues to be adapted and changed. This engagement included articulating for the school and district administration the deep connections that could be made between the school library redesign and the Winnetka School District's goal of expanding its STEAM program. By explicitly making the connections between the school library and the larger school district goals that are valued by most stakeholders, Burleson was able to "consistently [engage] with the school community to ensure that the school library resources, services, and standards align with the school's mission" (AASL 2018, School Library III.B.1.).

This engagement also led to gaining the buy-in of the larger community and created the opportunity for the Hubbard Woods School library to pilot the changes that could be made district-wide. This school librarian was able to put in motion changes and adjustments that would impact not just his school library but all the school libraries in the district, leading to change and innovation throughout the school system. Burleson created a detailed proposal for the school library space and presented it to the Hubbard Woods School Parent Teacher Organization (PTO). He used Google Drawings to create visuals so that PTO members could see the potential of the space and the opportunities that the new space would provide for learners. This visualization was key to the PTO members' better understanding of the changes and allowed Burleson to highlight possible future changes and adjustments to the school library as the space continues to evolve and as resources and technology evolve.

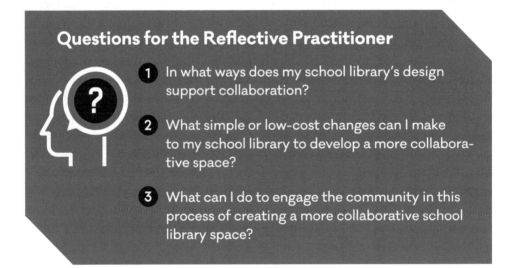

Questions for the Reflective Practitioner

1. In what ways does my school library's design support collaboration?

2. What simple or low-cost changes can I make to my school library to develop a more collaborative space?

3. What can I do to engage the community in this process of creating a more collaborative school library space?

8

Making Time and Space for Collaboration

he classroom educator begins with a story: "Imagine you are falling through the air. All around you are clouds rushing by, and wind whistles in your ears. . . . You pull hard at the handle gripped in your hand. There is a sharp tug and you slow down. Looking up, you see the wide silk canopy of a parachute opening above you. . . . You look down [and an] island is growing closer now and you begin to scan the shore. . . . You look up again, and all around you are the descending figures of . . . other members of your team, who have also come here to explore the dark interior of this strange and unknown island" (Taylor 2017, 11). The educator in this description is introducing the study of dinosaurs with her learners. The story she is telling is the beginning of an inquiry process in which learners participate as experts, and they are helping to guide the learning. As the unit of study goes on, learners will imagine themselves a team of experts who have traveled back in time to study dinosaurs. The learners will think about the equipment they will need, they will divide up into groups to focus on the discovering of different species of dinosaurs, and they will engage in research to learn about how the animals lived. The final steps might include a building project in which learners use what they have learned to create and share dioramas of the dinosaurs' habitats or organize and conduct a mock scientific conference in which they present their findings. This process is known as Imaginative Inquiry or Mantle of the Expert.

Mantle of the Expert is a teaching technique that incorporates drama and inquiry to create imaginary contexts for learning. This vehicle places the learners in the position of being an expert and the driver of the process and their learning. With this teaching process, "teachers work in collaboration with their students to generate

115

fictional settings that are used to study the curriculum and to develop knowledge, skills, and understanding across wide subject areas" (Taylor 2017, 13). During this process the educator creates a framework of the learning outcomes, uses dramatic prompts to create a sense of excitement with the learners, and places the learners in the position to help drive the inquiry and exploration of the subject matter. Mantle of the Expert incorporates storytelling devices and dramatic play to engage and empower learners to form questions and explore resources and offers a framework for the sharing of their findings in a way that celebrates their work.

Mantle of the Expert is a framework that needs flexibility and time, as does *all* learner-driven inquiry. Learners need space and time to engage in a process and really delve deep into a subject area to be able to inquire, think critically, collaborate, and learn. Lessons and units must have frameworks that allow learners time to learn, fail, design, and redesign their learning.

Connections with Collaboration and Time

The AASL Standards call for the school librarian to "[stimulate] learners to actively contribute to group discussions" (AASL 2018, School Librarian III.D.1.), "[develop] new understandings through engagement in a learning group" (AASL 2018, Learner III.A.2.), and "[lead] inquiry-based learning opportunities that enhance the information, media, visual, and technical literacies of all members of the school community" (AASL 2018, School Library III.A.2.). Developing all of these mindsets and competencies requires time. In thinking about the space that is provided for a school library, school librarians should think not just about the physical space allocated to the library but about the time that is provided in that space as well. For educators to provide inquiry-based learning opportunities for learners and to "[support] active learner participation" (AASL 2018, 85), time must be allotted so that learners can truly delve deeply into answering important questions and can explore a subject area, learn to do research using resources in a variety of different formats, and collaborate, create, and share new knowledge with an authentic audience, including other learners. Learners also need the opportunity to fail. Failure is an essential part of the learning process—in school and in life. Learners need the space and time to fail in information seeking, to rethink, and to pursue a different path to finding the understanding and knowledge that they are seeking. If schools and school librarians do not have the space and time in their curriculum for the inquiry process to flow and for failure and redesign to happen, then the goal of creating lifelong learners who Inquire, Include, Collaborate, Curate, Explore, and Engage will not be achievable.

If school librarians are to engage learners in a collaborative process, then learners need the time to work through the challenges and difficulties that arise when they do collaborate. Educators, including school librarians, must design projects and lessons that are not limited by arbitrary schedules and deadlines. Learners need to be able to pursue their passions and interests and the learning process. School librarians must work to develop lessons and projects that are open ended, that have a framework that outlines the goals and outcomes of the project, but that are not too tightly structured by the educator. When learners are given all the questions and all the resources, when every step is dictated and the final product already determined, then no inquiry, collaboration, or learner-driven learning is happening. School librarians need to cede some control of the process to the learners—facilitate the learning but not micromanage the learning. Mantle of the Expert is just one example of a teaching process with which school librarians and other educators can design a structure that meets the goals of the learning process but allows for collaboration and learner-driven inquiry.

COLLABORATE IN ACTION: GIVING LEARNERS TIME AND SPACE

The third graders at my school in Chicago study the history of the city of Chicago in a yearlong social studies unit. The central topic of Chicago starts with an exploration of the Indigenous Peoples who inhabited the land for generations before the migration of Western Europeans to the Midwest. The third graders learn about the western expansion that brought many Western Europeans to the land to settle and farm and about the eventual expansion of the city as transportation built up on the Great Lakes. Learners study the culture and life of the Ojibwe tribe and the connections to the land and environment. Next, they look at the major influx of immigrants to the city in the mid-1800s that changed Chicago into a large, metropolitan city of neighborhoods. Third graders learn about the Great Chicago Fire and the impact of that event on the design and architecture of the city. Learners study Hull House and the work of Jane Addams to provide social services to the city's immigrant populations. These learners also look at the neighborhoods of the city and learn about the impact of new populations on Chicago, including the Great Migration of African Americans from the segregated South to the South Side of Chicago. Learners study the impact of Chinese immigrants on the city after the racist laws of the western territories brought many new Asian immigrants to Chicago in the late 1800s and early 1900s, resulting in the founding of Chicago's Chinatown neighborhood. They study the changing population of the Pilsen neighborhood from Irish to Eastern European to Mexican immigrants as the city welcomed large populations from different parts of the world over the past 150 years of its history.

Think: Mapping a Yearlong Study

I have always supported this curriculum by providing books and resources and by teaching learners how to access information. However, I wanted to expand what I was doing and be able to have third graders "[develop] new understandings through engagement in a learning group" (AASL 2018, Learner III.A.2.). I worked with the technology education teacher and the third-grade teaching team to advocate for the administration's setting aside of a morning for professional development so everyone could look at the calendar and map out the learning. We advocated for this time by illustrating the benefits to the yearlong study for the school library and technology curriculum along with the benefits for learners from engaging in a more connected, deeper exploration of the classroom curriculum. The third-grade classroom educators shared how this planning time and connected study would also be beneficial to their own work as learners made deep connections to the history of the city in multiple areas of the school curriculum.

The professional development time was spent working with third-grade educators to learn more about the goals and outcomes of the study in their classrooms and then make deep connections with inquiry-based and learner-driven research, maker empowerment, and connections to a real-world challenge. The third-grade educators, the technology education teacher, and I designed a yearlong study that connected to the third-grade study of Chicago focusing on innovation in transportation at different points in the history of the city and making connections to the challenges currently facing the city. This process allowed me to design projects in the school library that would make deep connections to the classroom curriculum and to partner "with other educators to scaffold learning and organize learner groups to broaden and deepen understanding" (AASL 2018, School Library III.A.1.).

Mantle of the Expert was used as the framework for the inquiry and learning, allowing learners to be the drivers of the research and process with maker projects woven in. These maker projects focused on learners' coming up with their own ideas and building in a collaborative environment to demonstrate information they had collected. The yearlong project integrated various information-literacy skills, development of new knowledge, and collaborative building projects and allowed me to lead "inquiry-based learning opportunities that enhance the information, media, visual, and technical literacies of all members of the school community" (AASL 2018, School Library III.A.2.).

The third-grade educators, the technology education teacher, and I worked together to lay out the framework for the yearlong study. The project schedule reflected the timing for covering topics in the classroom. The subject areas included birchbark canoes used by the Ojibwe tribes; this topic was scheduled to align with the classroom study of the Indigenous Peoples. Later in the school year, third graders would learn in the school library about the creation of the elevated train system in Chicago while, at the same time, they would be studying the city during the late 1800s in their classrooms. At the end of the school year, in their library and technology time, learners would look at the current transportation systems in the city while they were studying the neighborhoods and maps of Chicago in their classrooms. The final challenge would involve learners in designing a transportation system for a Chicago of the future. This project would involve learners in thinking about everything that they learned about innovation in transportation throughout the history of Chicago, thinking about positive aspects of all these systems, and then thinking about environmental sustainability and equity of access to public transportation in the twenty-first century.

Think and Create: Inquiry and the Ojibwe Peoples

The framework of the project was focused on giving learners the opportunity to drive the inquiry and the learning while ensuring that the curricular goals and outcomes for learners were part of the design. The project started with third graders receiving a mysterious letter from Agent X informing them that X's agency was recruiting for a secret mission (figure 8.1). Applicants had to be curious, collaborative researchers and seekers of information. Learners recorded video applications in which they highlighted their skills and explained why they would be good collaborators. During the next session, learners received a mysterious package that contained images of paintings illustrating Ojibwe life, excerpts from journal entries from the 1820s when Western European people spent time with the Ojibwe, and pieces of birchbark. The letter instructed the third graders to document what they noticed in the images, journal entries, and bark and what they thought about these items, make factual connections to the pieces, and articulate what they wondered about the materi-

als. Learners were given a variety of resources from which to collect information; providing these resources and demonstrating their use were ways of "modeling the use of a variety of communication tools and resources" (AASL 2018, School Librarian III.B.1.).

Learners engaged in the See/Think/Wonder thinking routine as a way to drive the inquiry process. They made connections with the items and materials that they were given and documented the questions they had about the materials. Those questions were incorporated into the research process. This process also incorporated collaborative learning; learners talked to each other about the artifacts and shared their thoughts and ideas

FIGURE 8.1 / **Letter from Agent X**

as they documented their connections and questions. The collaborative sharing of materials, sharing of observations, and development of questions challenged "learners to work with others to broaden and deepen understandings" (AASL 2018, School Librarian III.A.1.). When learners were given a thinking routine framework and artifacts to study, they were empowered to make connections and spend time really looking at the materials, talking and sharing with each other and making connections with prior knowledge about the Ojibwe tribe and with new knowledge about birchbark canoes and the importance of transportation in society. The collaboration that happened with the third-grade educators and the timing of the classroom curriculum study of the Ojibwe tribe allowed me to coordinate the timing and sharing of these materials to ensure that I was able to scaffold "enactment of learning-group roles to enable the development of new understandings within a group" (AASL 2018, School Librarian III.A.2.).

Create: Mapping the Ojibwe Peoples and Birchbark Canoes

The third graders studied maps and talked about what they had learned about the importance of transportation to the Ojibwe people's way of life—for hunting and fishing, for traveling to find additional food sources, and for protection. Then the learners collaborated to create a shared Google Maps resource. They created markers in the Google Maps program and added facts and details about the Ojibwe people and connections to waterways. Learners also identified all the rivers and lakes in the area that the Ojibwe people might have used. This collaborative part of the project allowed me to "[model] the use of a variety of communication tools and resources" (AASL 2018, School Librarian III.B.1.). Through discussion and conversation, learners were asked to share information they collected and make connections between what they were learning from the study of the maps and what they were learning in their third-grade classrooms. This aspect of the project was also a way for me to cultivate "networks that allow learners to build on their own prior knowledge and create new knowledge" (AASL 2018, School Librarian III.B.2.) by creating a way for learners to build on the mapping skills they learned in the classroom, connect those skills to their study of birchbark canoes in the school library, and create a map to illustrate and share that knowledge. In this stage of the project, learners were not just using technology to collect information, they were creating a new piece of knowledge by creating a digital map that documented their learning and by sharing it with their classmates as they worked on this whole-grade-level project. The information-gathering stage of the project was allowed to progress as the learners explored different resources. The research had no set completion date. A framework and a schedule existed, but they were flexible and allowed the third graders the time and space they needed to collect the information, discuss it, and share their knowledge.

Think, Create, Share, and Grow: Building Canoes and New Knowledge

The next step in the project was a collaborative, hands-on building project whereby learners could experience the design aspect of canoes. The third graders were challenged to design and build a prototype of a birchbark canoe using only three materials: birchbark paper, craft sticks, and rubber cement. The birch paper was a connection to the birchbark used by the Ojibwe in the building of canoes, the craft sticks represented the wood that was used to maintain the structure of the canoe, and the rubber cement was a replacement for the sap that the Ojibwe used to seal the holes of the canoes. In addition to having the learners work in small groups, the goal was to have them really think about designing and building a product with a limited number of resources. This challenge made connections to the innovative nature of birchbark canoes and the deeper yearlong theme of innovation in transportation.

The design challenge in this project and a theme that was interwoven throughout the school year was one of maker empowerment. Maker empowerment is a concept of Agency by Design, a research arm of Project Zero at Harvard's Graduate School of Education. Maker empowerment is defined as "a heightened sensitivity to the made dimension of objects, ideas, and systems, along with a nudge toward tinkering with them and an increased capacity to do so" (Tishman 2013). The idea of maker empowerment is focused on understanding the human systems that surround learners—in this case, from the parts of the canoe to how those parts work together to allow the boat to float. When learners understand systems and the designs of systems, they can tinker with and rethink those designs to improve them or change them. When learners are empowered to design and make changes, they develop a mindset that they can be change makers in the world around them. The tinkering, designing, and prototyping processes of maker empowerment help to develop the skills of "[building] on . . . prior knowledge and [creating] new knowledge" (AASL 2018, Learner III.B.2.). When learners study and understand all the parts of a system, they then can be empowered to make positive changes to that system or create a new system or product.

The third graders were empowered to use the information they had learned about the building of the birchbark canoe and the features it needed to be useful to the Ojibwe people. Learners worked in pairs to create a collaborative design, negotiate, build a small prototype model of a canoe, and then test the model to see if it would hold material (in this case, small toy bricks and toy people) and stay afloat. This project created a structure for learners to "actively [contribute] to group discussions" (AASL 2018, Learner III.D.1.). The collaborative groups and the design process also allowed me to organize "learner groups for decision making and problem solving" (AASL 2018, School Librarian III.A.3.).

Throughout this process, educators worked only as facilitators. We did not dictate the design or process; learners were given the time and space to design, test, fail, and then redesign. Educators assisted with communication between partners, helping to negotiate and promote compromises when disagreements happened and lending an extra hand when needed in the building of the canoes. Through the process of helping learners negotiate and communicate, the third-grade educators and I were "demonstrating how to solicit and respond to feedback from others" (AASL 2018, School Librarian III.C.1.). In this part of the project, just as in the research process, a framework and schedule were established by the educators, but no hard deadline for learners to complete this project existed; again, they were given the time and space they needed to design, test, redesign, and test again.

All the groups were able to complete this project within the flexible schedule that was established by the educators. The fact that learners knew they would have the time that they needed resulted in focused groups who worked collaboratively but who were not constantly concerned with how much time they had left. The time and space that were given to the third graders to collaborate, create, fail, redesign, and create again are essential components of "advocating and modeling respect for diverse perspectives to guide the inquiry process" (AASL 2018, School Librarian III.C.2.), giving learners what they need to collect knowledge, listen to each other, and create new knowledge in a learner-led inquiry process.

Results of the Yearlong Transportation Study

The project continued throughout the school year with the third graders building on what they learned about the innovative nature of the birchbark canoes and then learning about the elevated train system, using the same framework of studying images, maps, and primary source documents from the inception of the train system until today. Learners worked collaboratively to continue to build on their prior knowledge by making connections to why a society would need a transportation system, from the Ojibwe to the expanding city of Chicago in the 1890s. Again, learners worked in pairs on a building project; in Tinkercad they designed the structural supports of the elevated train and 3-D printed them. Then they built the current elevated train system map using the 3-D structures and toy train tracks. The final challenges were to make connections to why a society needs a public transportation system and to use what they had learned from the past to design a transportation system for the future city of Chicago that considered innovation, environmental sustainability, and access for everyone in the city. The yearlong project was shared with the community throughout the school year. Articles about the birchbark canoe–building project were published in the all-school newsletter that is shared with the faculty, parents, and administration. The 3-D model of the elevated train system built by the third graders was displayed in the school library for learners in all the grade levels to see. The designs that learners created for the future city of Chicago transportation systems were shared by the learners in a whole-grade share-out. Learners also created a booklet with all their images and descriptions of their designs for environmentally sustainable and equitable transportation systems, and the booklet was shared with the mayor of the city of Chicago. Mayor Rahm Emanuel responded with a letter to the third graders thanking them for thinking about the future of the city.

This yearlong project integrated all aspects of the school library curriculum: developing and refining information-literacy skills, building knowledge and creating new knowledge, engaging in collaborative group work, and integrating technology and digital resources.

COLLABORATE IN ACTION: CREATING TIME AND SPACE FOR EDUCATOR COLLABORATION

The need for time extends beyond learners' need for time to drive the inquiry process, collaborate, and think about and rethink their process. Educators need time to collaborate, too. If school librarians and other educators are called on to "[lead] inquiry-based learning opportunities" (AASL 2018, School Library III.A.2.) and "[partner] . . . to scaffold learning and organize learner groups to broaden and deepen understanding" (AASL 2018, School Library III.A.1.), the thinking about and rethinking of these learning opportunities will require time to collaborate on the planning of the framework of the study, to reflect on the process, to make adjustments as the project progresses if reflections reveal the need, and, at the conclusion of the project, to refine it for the next year. The third-grade yearlong study was possible because the third-grade educators, the technology education teacher, and the school librarian asked for and were given the professional development time to plan the structure of the yearlong study and make connections with everyone's curriculum.

Reflections from the Principal

Kimeri Swanson-Beck is the head of the Lower School at the Francis W. Parker School where I am the school librarian. She was the administrator that the third-grade educators, the technology education teacher, and I approached to ask for the time to plan this project. Swanson-Beck reflected on the aspects of the project and the process we had shared to gain her approval for the time to coordinate and plan this project. She said that she needed answers to important questions to ensure that the project and the time that was given would be in service to the curricula of the three departments (third grade, school library, and technology education) and to the mission and goals of the school.

Swanson-Beck also reflected on her support of the open-ended nature of the project. The facts that the project did not have a strict time frame for each step and was driven by the inquiry process of the learners fit with the mission and focus of the Francis W. Parker School. She said that fit was an important part of her support for this project. Parker is a progressive education school, and the mission of the school is focused on educating learners for the world that they live in now. Swanson-Beck

Questions for Approval of Collaborative Planning Time

Kimeri Swanson-Beck, head of the Lower School at the Francis W. Parker School, considers the following questions when reviewing educators' proposals for curriculum changes and requests for administration approval for educator workshop days connected to curricular changes.

1. What are the benefits to the learners? What ways will learners grow through this experience?

2. How is the project evaluated? What is the assessment process? Is there a grade or rubric that all educators involved will follow?

3. Is everyone (classroom educators, departmental educators) on board with this project?

4. What roles will all the educators involved in this project take on to ensure that the project meets the goals?

5. How will the project make connections with the curriculum of all departments and advance all curricula?

6. What is the impact to the grade below or above the grade level that is engaging in this project? How does the project advance the learner goals that were developed in the lower grade and prepare learners for the next grade?

7. What is the cost? This includes funding for any supplies, additional curricular materials, and overtime or supplemental pay for educators' time.

8. How will this project be shared with the school community, other learners, and educators in the school or beyond to be a model for other grade levels or departments?

said, "This project gave students the chance to take skills they developed and test them in an authentic way." Learners were challenged to take what they learned about the history of the innovation of transportation in Chicago and design and build an innovative transportation system that would provide a sustainable, equitable system for the future Chicago, a current issue facing the city. Swanson-Beck also reflected that the framework of the project provided concrete connections with the curricula of the classroom, the school library, and the technology education department while also allowing learners to pursue their interests and passions and to experience the joy and fun of learning. "Developing lifelong lovers of learning is an important part of the mission of the school," said Swanson-Beck. For the learners to really have an authentic learning experience that met the goals of collaborating, giving and receiving feedback, and engaging in an iterative design process, the third graders needed time and space to work through the process. "The team was able to clearly illustrate why the open-ended nature of the project was essential to the learners' experience and skills development," stated Swanson-Beck. For school librarians advocating for administrative support for collaborative planning time, Swanson-Beck suggested, "Think about what the mission and goals of your school are and make sure your pitch has concrete connections to them." School librarians need to engage "with the school community to ensure that the school library resources, services, and standards align with the school's mission" (AASL 2018, School Library III.B.1.).

Reflections from a Third-Grade Educator

Amy Przygoda is a third-grade educator at the Francis W. Parker School. She was one of the educators who took part in the collaborative design of this project. Przygoda reflected on the benefits of this project in meeting her curricular goals and in developing her learners' collaboration skills. Concerning the planning and design of the project, she reflected that sharing the teaching materials with the whole team of educators was essential to ensuring that the project met her classroom goals while also allowing the technology education teacher and me to bring in new materials and perspectives for the third graders, helping learners expand their knowledge and understanding. Przygoda also said that the collaboration with other educators on this project allowed everyone to bring their ideas and strengths to the project, thereby creating a more meaningful and deeper project for the learners. When thinking about the assessment process, she said, "There were more adults engaged in this process and observing students, giving new perspective and assessments of the learners, leading to a more complete view of learners in different learning situations."

Przygoda said that reflection and flexibility were essential to the success of the open-ended framework of the project. "We were always checking in with each other, either over e-mail and the shared calendar [table 8.1] or in person between classes to see where students were in the process, what was working, and what had to be adjusted." Flexibility on the part of everyone involved was essential; because the project was learner-driven, educators had to be open to the schedule evolving as the project progressed. "Trusting each other was so important. I needed to trust that even if I didn't totally know what was happening with the canoe building, that the other teachers did and that everyone had the students' learning experience as the goal of this project," reflected Przygoda. This process highlights how school librarians can partner "with other educators to scaffold learning and organize learner groups to broaden and deepen understanding" (AASL 2018, School Library III.A.1.).

Providing the time and space for learners to engage in the inquiry process and build new knowledge was possible because of the collaboration between the school librarian and fellow educators. The willingness of all the educators to collaborate, listen to, and work with each other in the yearlong study of Chicago was essential for the curriculum to be a success. Sharing resources, staying in communication, making connections with the classroom and school library curricula, and develop-

TABLE 8.1 /
Shared calendar

Classroom	Third-Grade Classroom 1	Third-Grade Classroom 2	Third-Grade Classroom 3
Integrated Learning and Information Sciences (ILIS) Tech	Google Maps neighborhood mapping activity: learners map their route to and from school and then print out the map	Google Maps neighborhood mapping activity: learners map their route to and from school and then print out the map	Google Maps neighborhood mapping activity: learners map their route to and from school and then print out the map
ILIS Tech	Technology device distribution for work in classrooms; let Sarah and Seth know if you need support	Google Maps neighborhood mapping activity: learners map their route to and from school and then print out the map	Fire drill scheduled so shortened time; devices available for classroom work if needed
ILIS Library	Learners check out books and create 3-D comics and book recommendations	Learners check out books and create 3-D comics and book recommendations	Learners check out books and create 3-D comics and book recommendations
ILIS Tech	Kickoff of collaborative project: focus on imaginative component, reading of letter from Agent X, and intro of challenge; meets in the library	No school—County Fair	Kickoff of collaborative project: focus on imaginative component, reading of letter from Agent X, and intro of challenge; meets in the library
ILIS Tech	Technology device distribution for work in classrooms; let Sarah and Seth know if you need support	Envelope of artifacts for students to explore in See/Think/Wonder activity; meets in the library	Envelope of artifacts for students to explore in See/Think/Wonder activity; meets in the library
ILIS Library	Envelope of artifacts for students to explore in See/Think/Wonder activity; meets in the library	Kickoff of collaborative project: focus on imaginative component, reading of letter from Agent X, and intro of challenge; meets in the library	Third-Grade Classroom 3 on a field trip
ILIS Tech	No school—Fall weekend	Research exploration; meets in the library	Brain Pop—Ice Age
ILIS Tech	Research exploration; meets in the library	Technology device distribution for work in classrooms; let Sarah and Seth know if you need support	Research exploration; meets in the library
ILIS Library	Research exploration; meets in the library	Research exploration; meets in the library	Research exploration; meets in the library

ing a trusting relationship between the classroom educators and the school librarian highlight how to "[create] and [maintain] a learning environment that supports and stimulates discussion from all members of the school community" (AASL 2018, School Library III.D.1.).

Questions for the Reflective Practitioner

1. In what ways is my school library giving learners the time and space they need to become collaborators?

2. How can I connect with other educators to allow learners the time and space they need to make deep connections to the curriculum?

3. In what ways can I and other school librarians advocate for other educators and school administrators to support providing time and space for learners to grow as collaborators?

Conclusion: Drawing Connections between the Shared Foundations

A collaborative mindset is not a skill that can be developed in isolation—from other learners nor from other Shared Foundations in the AASL Standards. Collaboration is about listening, thinking critically, engaging with others, bringing different ideas and perspectives together, and then designing and redesigning based on outcomes. When school librarians are working to develop a collaborative mindset in learners and other educators, their planning and teaching should be done in the context of all six Shared Foundations. Just as the Competencies and Alignments of Collaborate for learners, school librarians, and school libraries should be envisioned as intersecting in a Venn diagram, so, too, should the interconnected nature of the Shared Foundations be recognized. When school librarians plan for incorporating the AASL Standards into their work, they must see the Shared Foundations as intersecting and intertwining with each other and not as separate outcomes.

Thinking about Collaborate in the context of all the other Shared Foundations makes it possible to see the deep thinking and deep connections that can result when school librarians create a collaborative, inquiry-based, learner-centered environment in the school library and in the whole school. I encourage all school librarians to take time to step back from the daily demands on their time and view all the Shared Foundations from twenty thousand feet to see the whole learning landscape and how all the Shared Foundations influence teaching and learning.

Inquire

The Shared Foundation of Inquire calls for learners to "build new knowledge by inquiring, thinking critically, identifying problems, and developing strategies for solving problems" (AASL 2018, 34). Developing inquiry skills and building new knowledge cannot happen in isolation. Learners need to work with others to find information that helps learners construct new knowledge. Talking and listening to others require the mindset of Collaborate and recognition of the social nature of information seeking. In collaboration, learners build the skills of listening and being open to new perspectives and voices, as well as recognizing when voices are missing from the inquiry process, bringing the Shared Foundation of Include into the mix. The social learning of inquiry is intertwined with the social learning of collaboration. When learners are asked to problem-solve, a key is understanding what the problem is and how that problem impacts others, gaining empathy for someone else. Working with others is essential for learners to better understand the problem. Collaboration is key to success when building "new knowledge by inquiring, thinking critically, identifying problems, and developing strategies for solving problems" (AASL 2018, 34).

Include

The Shared Foundation of Include calls for learners to "demonstrate an understanding of and commitment to inclusiveness and respect for diversity in the learning community" (AASL 2018, 35). Learners who are inclusive and respect diversity in the learning process also have the mindset of Collaborate and the ability to "work effectively with others to broaden perspectives and work toward common goals" (AASL 2018, 36). School librarians are "advocating and modeling respect for diverse perspectives to guide the inquiry process" (AASL 2018, School Librarian III.C.2.). In order for learners to have respect for diverse perspectives, learners need to understand how to listen and how to recognize what voices are missing from their learning—a Competency that may involve inquiry to determine who else has a voice that can inform learning. In collaboration, learners develop the skills to "[establish] connections with other learners to build on their own prior knowledge and create new knowledge" (AASL 2018, Learner III.B.2.). A commitment to inclusiveness is a commitment to listen to others and incorporate their perspectives in the new knowledge that learners are creating. A collaborative mindset is essential to that success.

Curate

The Shared Foundation of Curate calls on learners to "make meaning for oneself and others by collecting, organizing, and sharing resources of personal relevance" (AASL 2018, 37). Learners must be able to evaluate sources and collect information from a diverse set of resources. They also need to "respect the ideas and backgrounds of others" (AASL 2018, 96). When learners have the qualities of a collaborator, they know that diverse perspectives are essential to "[working] productively with others to solve problems" (AASL 2018, Learner III.C.). Collaborators "[recognize] learning as a social responsibility" (AASL 2018, Learner III.D.2.). In order for learners to be both collaborators and curators of information and new knowledge, they must recognize the need to connect with others. When learners have the qualities of a collaborator, they are open to those voices and perspectives. Because learners who collaborate have as part of their learning experience listening to others and soliciting feedback from others, they know that being open to feedback will lead to better understanding and a more effective selection of resources to curate. When learners effectively Curate, they understand the need to "collaborate with others, either in person or with a larger learning community through technology, to integrate their own knowledge with the information of others" (AASL 2018, 96). Learning from others is essential to both Collaborate and Curate—one cannot be done without the other.

Explore

Under the Explore Shared Foundation, learners "discover and innovate in a growth mindset developed through experience and reflection" (AASL 2018, 38). When learners are asked to challenge themselves and be lifelong learners always growing and rethinking their ideas and designs, being open to feedback and reflection is an essential key to success. The Collaborate Competencies call on learners to engage in learning groups, connect with other learners to build on their own knowledge, and solicit and respond to feedback from others (AASL 2018, 84). The Explore Competencies recognize that in order for learners to "discover and innovate," they must "become part of and engage with the larger learning community" (AASL 2018, 106). Learners must have opportunities to "collaboratively brainstorm various investigation strategies and develop innovative solutions for critical problem-solving tasks" (AASL 2018, 106). Learners with a collaborative mindset "[develop] new understandings through engagement in a learning group" (AASL 2018, Learner III.A.2.) and "[decide] to solve problems informed by group interaction" (AASL 2018, Learner III.A.3.). If school librarians are calling on learners to discover and innovate in order to grow as lifelong learners, then learners need to possess the ability to listen to and engage with other learners and be open to the feedback from others to rethink and redesign their work. To Explore and Collaborate, learners must "[recognize] learning as a social responsibility" (AASL 2018, Learner III.D.2.), and to grow as lifelong learners, they must be open to learning from others.

Engage

In the Shared Foundation of Engage, learners are called on to "demonstrate safe, legal, and ethical creating and sharing of knowledge products independently while engaging in a community of practice and an interconnected world" (AASL 2018, Learner VI.). This Shared Foundation recognizes that learners need to be engaged in the ethical sharing of knowledge while understanding that even individual work has community and social aspects in our interconnected world. Sharing knowledge includes understanding how to search for and find information from reliable and reputable sources and developing the skills to ethically credit and share that information. Learners also need to understand the impact that sharing information has on their learning community and on the larger interconnected world. Learners always need to be aware of "learning as a social responsibility" (AASL 2018, Learner III.D.2.) and to understand that they, as creators of new knowledge, are responsible as citizens to ethically and legally share their work and the work of others. Collaborators understand that all learning is social and that knowledge is shared—understandings that are essential in the global society in which they live.

The Big Picture

As school librarians consider the Shared Foundation of Collaborate, keeping the big picture in mind is essential—the view from twenty thousand feet. When developing the mindset of Collaborate, school librarians must reflect on and think about the interconnected nature of all the Shared Foundations. Documenting all these mindset developments should be consistent across school libraries, districts, and grade levels to ensure that all learners are engaging in this work to develop mindsets mapped out in all six Shared Foundations. None of the foundations should be looked at in isolation and documented independently. Instead, they should be viewed as interconnected mindsets and Competencies that work together and lead to learners who are better equipped to meet the challenges of the twenty-first century, its technology, and essential information-literacy skills.

Collaboration is a complex skill that is not developed in isolation. Developing the mindset of Collaborate in learners is intertwined with growing a culture of collaboration between school librarians and fellow educators and cultivating a culture of collaboration in the school library space. As learners, school librarians, and fellow educators engage in collaborative work, they flow in and out of the Domains of Think, Create, Share, and Grow. While collaboration is happening, the other AASL Shared Foundations are happening as well. All the Shared Foundations, Key Commitments, Domains, Competencies, and Alignments are interconnected and complex. When learners of all ages, including educators, are given opportunities to grow in a learning environment that recognizes these intersections, then all learners are empowered "to pursue academic and personal success" (AASL 2018, 12) as engaged members of the global society.

Works Cited

AASL American Association of School Librarians. 2018. *National School Library Standards for Learners, School Librarians, and School Libraries.* Chicago, IL: ALA Editions.

Barrett, Peter, Yufan Zhang, Fay Davies, and Lucinda Barrett. 2015. *Clever Classrooms: Summary Report of the HEAD Project (Holistic Evidence and Design).* Manchester, England: University of Salford.

Cassel, Sean. 2018. "Simple Relationship-Building Strategies." Edutopia, George Lucas Educational Foundation. www.edutopia.org/article/simple-relationship-building-strategies.

Clapp, Edward P., et al. 2017. *Maker-Centered Learning: Empowering Young People to Shape Their Worlds.* San Francisco: Jossey-Bass.

Curtin, Melanie. 2018. "10 Skills Employers Will Want the Most in 2020." *Business Insider,* January 4. www.businessinsider.com/10-skills-employers-will-want-the-most-in-2020-2018-1.

"Design Thinking." 2019. IDEO U. www.ideou.com/pages/design-thinking.

D'Onfro, Jillian. 2015. "The Truth about Google's Famous '20% Time' Policy." *Business Insider,* April 17. www.businessinsider.com/google-20-percent-time-policy-2015-4.

Fisher, Anna V., Karrie E. Godwin, and Howard Seltman. 2014. "Visual Environment, Attention Allocation, and Learning in Young Children: When Too Much of a Good Thing May Be Bad." *Psychological Science, 25*(7), 1362–1370. doi:10.1177/0956797614533801.

frog. n.d. Collective Action Toolkit. www.frogdesign.com/work/frog-collective-action-toolkit.

"Get Started!" 2019. International Dot Day: Get Started! Reynolds Center for Teaching, Learning, and Creativity. www.thedotclub.org/dotday/get-started.

Gross-Loh, Christine. 2016. "How Praise Became a Consolation Prize." *Atlantic,* December 16. www.theatlantic.com/education/archive/2016/12/how-praise -became-a-consolation-prize/510845/.

Harvard Project Zero. n.d. "See Think Wonder Routine." Visible Thinking. http:// www.visiblethinkingpz.org/VisibleThinking_html_files/03_ThinkingRoutines/ 03c_Core_routines/SeeThinkWonder/SeeThinkWonder_Routine.html.

An Introduction to Design Thinking: Process Guide. n.d. Stanford, CA: Hasso Plattner Institute of Design at Stanford. https://dschool-old.stanford.edu/sandbox/ groups/designresources/wiki/36873/attachments/74b3d/ModeGuideBOOT CAMP2010L.pdf.

"Investigating Where We Live: Washington, DC." 2019. National Building Museum. www.nbm.org/exhibition/investigating-where-we-live/.

Kaplan, Kate. 2016. "When and How to Create Customer Journey Maps." Fremont, CA: Nielsen Norman Group. www.nngroup.com/articles/customer-journey -mapping.

Kesler, Chris. 2019. "What Is Genius Hour?" Genius Hour. geniushour.com/what -is-genius-hour/.

Martin, Katie. 2018. *Learner-Centered Innovation: Spark Curiosity, Ignite Passion and Unleash Genius.* IMPress.

National Novel Writing Month (NaNoWriMo). 2019. "About." nanowrimo.org/ about.

O'Donnell Wicklund Pigozzi and Peterson. 2010. *The Third Teacher: 79 Ways You Can Use Design to Transform Teaching and Learning.* New York: Abrams.

"Our Organization." n.d. TED: Ideas Worth Spreading. www.ted.com/about/ our-organization.

Out of Eden Learn. n.d. "About Us." Project Zero, Harvard Graduate School of Education. learn.outofedenwalk.com/about/.

Simon, Nina. 2010. *The Participatory Museum.* Santa Cruz, NM: Museum 2.0.

Taylor, Tim. 2017. *A Beginner's Guide to Mantle of the Expert: A Transformative Approach to Education.* Norwich, England: Singular Publishing.

Tishman, Shari. 2013. "Maker Empowerment: A Concept under Construction." *Agency by Design* (blog). www.agencybydesign.org/node/335.

About the Author

MARY CATHERINE COLEMAN is a Lower and Intermediate School librarian at the Francis W. Parker School in Chicago, Illinois. She earned her master's degree in library and information sciences from Dominican University in River Forest, Illinois, and has worked in public and school libraries for the past fourteen years. Coleman is the 2017 recipient of the AASL Collaborative School Library Award. She has presented at local, national, and international conferences on school library programming, maker empowerment, and collaboration in school libraries. Coleman documents her work on her blog *The Reimagined Library* at https://thereimaginedlibrary.blogspot.com.

Index

An italicized page number indicates an illustration or table.

3-D printing, 122
20 percent time, 71

A
AASL Standards Framework for Learners, xii
AASL Standards Framework for School
    Librarians, xii
AASL Standards Framework for School Libraries,
    xiii
AASL Standards in action. *See* alignments
    for school libraries; competencies
    for learners; competencies for school
    librarians
AASL Standards Integrated Framework,
    intersections within, *xvii*
active listening. *See* listening skills
adaptability (human), 34, 35, 45, 47
adaptability (library space and furnishings),
    106–110, 111–112, 113
advocacy for school library, 15, 20, 30, 40
affective domain of learning. *See* Share Domain
    in Collaborate Shared Foundation
alignments for school libraries
    Collaborate Shared Foundation
        Create Domain, xiii, 7, 15, 24, 30, 32, 35, 39,
            109, 114, 125
        Grow Domain, xiii, 4, 12, 15, 22, 39, 40, 41,
            106, 107, 109, 111, 112, 113
        Share Domain, xiii, 3–4, 12, 20, 38, 40, 108,
            113
        Think Domain, xiii, 5, 18, 25, 39, 65, 104,
            113, 116, 118, 123, 125
    Curate Shared Foundation, 104, 131

Engage Shared Foundation, 46, 48, 49, 59, 132
Explore Shared Foundation, 116, 131–132
Include Shared Foundation, 15, 130
Inquire Shared Foundation, 116, 130
art and literature project focusing on process
    over product, 68–71
assessment of learners
    by classroom educators, 14, 125. *See* also
        documenting learner process and
        progress
    by peers, 54–55, 56–57, 59, 116
    by school librarian, 7, 15, 24, 35–36, 78, 80,
        89–90, 125
assessment of learners' needs, 13
audience
    for documenting learning, 14. *See* also
        authentic audience for sharing learning
        products
    for testing lesson plan, 10
authentic audience for sharing learning
    products, 24, 71, 75, 95, 97, 99, 116,
    122–123
authentic feedback. *See* feedback
autism. *See* sensory story time

B
Back of the Yards Coffee Co. project, 95–99
Beebe, Sarah, 51–55
Bee-Bot robots, 20–21
benefits
    of collaboration, 15, 18–19, 41, 93, 109, 124,
        125
    of curation, 131
    of engagement, 132
    of exploration, 131–132
    of inclusion, 130

space for collaborative learning, 73–75, 103–114, 115–127
spreading collaboration, 40, 94–99
stakeholders
   communicating with, 13, 31–32, 35, 122–123, 124
   participating in planning and decision making, 7, 35–36, 38, 109, 110, 113–114
   respected in vision for school library, 34–35
   supporting school library, 109
storytelling, 6, 20, 24, 47–50, 59, 60–61, 68–70, 116
storytelling sequence lesson, 20–21
Swanson-Beck, Kimeri, 123–125

T
Tabor, Kate, 68–71
technology integration examples
   3-D printing, 122
   audio recording, 23–24
   BuzzFeed, 70–71
   coding, 22–24
   computer interface, 22–25, 25–27
   Cricut cutter, 50
   drawing application, 50
   drawing software, 50
   LittleBits circuits, 63
   mapping application, 120
   motors, 26
   robots, 20–21, 63
   shared cloud drives, 72, 74
   social media, 58, 71, 99
   Tinkercad, 122
   video creation tool, 74, 119
TED model, 29
Test step of design thinking process, 54–55
Think Domain in Collaborate Shared Foundation
   alignments for school libraries, xiii, 5, 18, 25, 39, 65, 104, 113, 116, 118, 123, 125

competencies for learners, xii, 47, 48, 49, 61, 65, 72, 73–74, 75, 79, 82, 86, 92, 96, 116, 118
competencies for school librarians, xii, 6, 21, 33, 63, 69–70, 120, 121
examples of Think activities
   educators, 6, 20, 24, 32, 39, 117
   learners, 47–49, 50–51, 62–65, 69–71, 72, 81, 82, 86, 88, 89, 91, 92, 96, 98, 119–121
Third Teacher, 104
time for learners to collaborate, 70, 115–122
time for planning collaborative instruction
   getting administrative support, 7, 118, 123–125
   as motivator for educators, 7, 12
Tinkercad, 122
tolerance. *See* diverse perspectives
transportation study, 118–119, 122–123
trust, 26, 27, 67, 125, 127
   See also relationship building
Twitter, 71

V
viewpoints. *See* diverse perspectives
vision and values statement, 32
visual environment's effect on learners, 105–106
voice and choice for learners, 7, 12–13, 51, 67–76
   See also lesson examples

W
weeding to improve library space, 105–106, 111
welcoming space (school library), 104, 108, 109–110, 113
work readiness. *See* career readiness, school librarians' contribution to
Wurman, Richard Saul, 29